BEHAVECON

A REVEALING GUIDE TO OUTSMARTING YOURSELF, MAKING THE BEST DECISIONS & LEADING THE RICHEST LIFE

JAN DOMINIK GUNKEL

2014

BEHAVECON
Print Edition – other formats available
Copyright: Jan Dominik Gunkel
Published: 17 June 2014, First Edition
First Printing: June 2014
Printed in the United States of America
ISBN: 978-0-615-92159-4
Publisher: Inupio GmbH, Mendig, Germany

For my parents, Karl and Doris Gunkel,
and everyone who wants to make this world a better
place.

Building a better future
Ten percent of all author royalties are donated to
scientific research and education at leading institutions
worldwide during at least the first three calendar years
after publication.

Gratitude

My parents, who taught me to live.

Grandma, for teaching me the meaning of work ethic (oh and I needed loads of it while writing this).

All the amazing stories, studies, and tips you will find in this book are thanks to numerous experts, researchers, and individuals who have devoted lifetimes of exhausting labor to this subject. I am lucky to have been able to speak to a few of them and proud to have read so much of their findings. The present work was only made possible by them laying the foundation, as well as by all the proofreaders, critics, and editors who made their significant contributions. If you encounter something too crazy, stupid, or plain wrong in this book, that's me not having listened to their advice.

Here is a list of inspiring giants whom I would like to thank up front as I was so deeply impressed by their works. This content, as well as my life, builds so much on their findings (in alphabetical order—many more can be found in the reference section at the end of this book):

- Dan Ariely
- Leo Babauta
- Edward de Bono

- Peter Drucker
- Michael Ellsberg
- Tim Ferriss
- Malcolm Gladwell
- Daniel Kahneman
- Dacher Keltner
- Barbara and Allan Pease
- Ramit Sethi
- Richard Thaler
- Amos Tversky
- Paul Slovic
- Jack Welch

My friends who carefully read and discussed this book: Aaron M. Shepherd, Bastian Kluck, Jimmy Tomczak, Lindsay Kennedy James, Reiner M. Hillbricht, and Thomas Klein.

Nils Zuendorf and Suparni Neuwirth for creating and executing the promotion strategy.

Many friends and acquaintances, the readers of my blog and Twitter feed, for their comments and ongoing encouragement.

Thank you, all; you are amazing! You make my days!

CONTENTS

Supporting material can be found at
http://www.behavecon.com/supportingmaterial.xls

START HERE

In this part...

To get going you figure out what this book is all about and how to use it. You get a better sense of the life you could lead and the irrationalities we are all facing. Finally, I introduce myself so you can acquaint yourselves a bit to the person that I truly am. Turn the page to get real. What follows are not some superstitious ideas but precise scientific decisions guidelines, based on studies and hard facts. Learn what you have got inside.

Jan Dominik Gunkel

You, Your Life, and This Book

"Most people are, by definition, ordinary. Yet more than half
of a group of college graduates surveyed said they plan to be
millionaire by the age of forty."
— Ramit Sethi
American financial adviser

"I see no reason to have my shirts ironed. It's irrational."
— Barry Commoner
1980 US presidential candidate

Introduction

Do you deserve more from your life? More quality?
More riches? More time?

Would you like to have more money but cannot
make more in your job? Also, you cannot or do not
want to work more?

Do you see your friends bragging about all the
things they have, and you feel like you are the Jone$es'
neighbor?

Are you afraid to even think about a vacation
because you can never afford it? (If so, you are part of
the 33% of Americans who said they had no spare cash
in the past holiday season.)

Would you like to understand where Madison Avenue is going in its arms race against Main Street?[1] And how you are being influenced and tricked into financial decisions?

Do you already know how to keep track of your checkbook — and you are saving money, you are working hard, but still you just do not seem to get rich?

If you answered yes to most of these questions, you have picked the right book.

Bad news right up front: Everything looks like it will get worse. Nobel laureate Joseph E. Stiglitz predicts that "because of the choices that have already been made, the downturn be far longer and deeper than necessary but also we will emerge from the crisis with a much larger legacy of debt, with a financial system that is less competitive, less efficient and more vulnerable to another crisis and with an economy less prepared to meet the challenges of this century." We have to ready ourselves for a rough ride.

Our new world will demand a host of new skills as the "debt financed consumption binge supported by [the] housing bubble" is no longer there to fuel our expenses. In this book, I am going to teach you to understand and transform your decisions so that you can gain the financial independence you have been dreaming of.

---

[1] Madison Avenue is the street in Manhattan famous for all its marketing firms.

What Is the Life You Want to Lead?

When we think about living a larger life, living a better life, most of us immediately think more money. So let us look at who the rich people really are in the United States. A study found that 40% of millionaires are so-called satisfied savers and secret succeeders. These people became rich by being frugal and investing well, and they keep up their lifestyle. They are not hotel heiresses or movie stars. In fact, they are welding contractors, pharmacists, and pest controllers. Their insignia are not Lamborghinis but used cars and inexpensive Quartz watches, not Rolex. Once you have made it, you don't need to prove it to anyone anymore. You might as well stop trying to prove it.

Rich means spending power. It means being able to afford pretty much anything you want. Whether that is a sports car, a trip around the world in luxury hotels, or the latest and greatest fashion. Or time with friends, family, and yourself. However, it means also having that power without going out and using it all the time. It is as much about money as it is about self-control. It is about making the right decisions and sticking to them.

Living a great life is knowing your true desires and being able to fulfill them, while not wasting your energy and money chasing illusions. It is having that little extra money—always. And there is much more we can attain once we have the basic financial security established that allows us the further pursuit of our dreams. Check out the pictured Holstee Company Manifesto as an example of a value statement that has been resonating with many people lately. You will see that at its core, it is full of decisions and actions, not money.

THIS IS YOUR **LIFE.**
DO WHAT YOU LOVE,
AND DO IT OFTEN.
IF YOU DON'T LIKE SOMETHING, CHANGE IT.
IF YOU DON'T LIKE YOUR JOB, QUIT.
IF YOU DON'T HAVE ENOUGH TIME, STOP WATCHING TV.
IF YOU ARE LOOKING FOR THE LOVE OF YOUR LIFE, STOP;
THEY WILL BE WAITING FOR YOU WHEN YOU
START DOING THINGS YOU LOVE.
STOP OVER ANALYZING, ALL EMOTIONS ARE BEAUTIFUL.
WHEN YOU EAT, APPRECIATE
LIFE IS SIMPLE. EVERY LAST BITE.
OPEN YOUR MIND, ARMS, AND HEART TO NEW THINGS
AND PEOPLE, WE ARE UNITED IN OUR DIFFERENCES.
ASK THE NEXT PERSON YOU SEE WHAT THEIR PASSION IS,
AND SHARE YOUR INSPIRING DREAM WITH THEM.
TRAVEL OFTEN; GETTING LOST WILL
HELP YOU FIND YOURSELF.
SOME OPPORTUNITIES ONLY COME ONCE, SEIZE THEM.
LIFE IS ABOUT THE PEOPLE YOU MEET, AND
THE THINGS YOU CREATE WITH THEM
SO GO OUT AND START CREATING.
LIFE IS LIVE YOUR DREAM
SHORT. AND SHARE
YOUR PASSION.

"THE HOLSTEE MANIFESTO" ©2009   WRITTEN BY DAVE, MIKE & FABIAN   DESIGN BY RACHAEL   WWW.HOLSTEE.COM/MANIFESTO

So take a couple of minutes and jot down a list of what you would like your life to look like. Why would you like to be richer?

Would you like to have more time to spend with your partner? Or have time to find the one? Are you craving for the money to hire a private dancing trainer? What about off-loading all the household chores? Never cleaning again? Having a gardener? Or would you like to have the time and money to get a university degree—for yourself or your kids? Go on a sailing trip? Wear fancy designer clothes? Travel? Learn about other cultures? Lie under the sun? There are so many things you might seek. List them. List them all and imagine them vividly. This list should be a good reason to read this book and give you the sense of purpose in many of your activities.

What Is This Book?

You will explore why we chose what we chose and how we can change our behavior to choose what we actually want without involuntarily going astray. Before we get there, however, we will have a look at where we stand in life and what we really want. By learning this, you can rid yourself of the bonds of modern slavery and enjoy a new and rare freedom.

In the past, a whole trade was built on the presumed fact that people are rational. Nowadays, people expect rationality in others and in themselves. The trade I am referring to is economics. Yet as we have become increasingly aware, we are not rational. I am not, and neither are you. In fact, it is believed today that 80% of our decisions are emotionally based rather than rationally based. Science has developed behavioral economics to take this into account. This is in part due to technological advances that spawned the field of neuroscience. Here we learn about brain structure and activity with modern brain monitoring systems, so-called EEGs and fMRIs. Together with the advances in psychology, neuropsychology was born. Finally, by combining neuropsychology and economics, we start to understand what drives our decisions. Decisions we have been making for centuries. By trial and error, generations have devised ways to make their products stick, get us to buy what we do not need, pay inflated prices, and deal with issues of daily life. Our lifestyle has developed over centuries without us truly comprehending our desires. Now, by means of this new science, we can make great leaps by understanding what drives us and our fellow people. All statements made in this book are backed by scientific research, as you can see in the appendix or by personal experience.

You can learn to uncover the ploys, live the life you desire at a price you can afford. This will bring new meaning to your life and allow you to focus on your real priorities. After all, life is not all about money but about all the other blessings, friendships, love, and fun. The following pages will help you build this understanding and guide you with a set of tools step-by-step toward a financial strength and willpower you have never had. It will leave you with a toolkit to build a foundation strong enough to pursue dreams that once were beyond your reach. That is my promise.

It will be hard work, so be prepared, as this is not just theory but also practical application. The tricks in this book have saved me tens of thousands of dollars and have the potential for even more. So I would say they are well worth investing a little time and effort.

Who Is This Book For?

The only prerequisite I ask of you: a sane and open mind. I will be telling you things about yourself, and you might feel bad about them. You are in good company. Many readers feel this way, and I have not fully mastered all of these either. Let this be the manifesto for your change for the better. Embrace it and make small changes every day.

No special talents or aptitudes are required. Nature endowed you with all you need. You can get started anywhere in life. This book is written to make you win and understand how to do so — consistently.

Side note: Depending on where you are at financially, reading this book and applying its learnings might not be enough. Just changing the behavior that got you there might not be sufficient to get you back out again. So if you are in deep trouble, advice specific to your situation might be a sensible addition.

My Story

It's about making decisions and sticking to them. If there is one thing I pride myself in excelling at, it is the ability to turn things in my life around entirely. For example, until the age of 20, I did not even know how to spell *sports*. I was a lazy kid that figured out a way to be exempted from all school sports. Fast-forward a decade. Today I participate in runs, and I easily swim two miles in under an hour. I am healthy and, more important, feel as though I am at the pinnacle of physical fitness.

Until age 30, I was not able to get up early a single day a year without pain. Today, I am an early riser. And I have to be — in part because of this book. As a successful businessman managing a global division of a large company, I have to find time to write these lines. And in the morning before I go to work, I spend a couple of hours researching and doing so.

So where does that discipline come from? Discipline is two things: It is a strong will at times, but it is even more a sense of cleverness, an understanding of how our psyche works so we can outsmart it. Getting ahead of your inner Schweinehund.[2]

Back in 2008, a friend of mine suggested I read Dan Ariely's book *Predictably Irrational*. As I have always been extremely ambitious, it did not take long for me to realize that behavioral economics is the ticket to becoming the man I wanted to be. Since then, I have developed a keen interest in "behavecon," as I like to call it. (Whether you pronounce it "behav-econ" or "behave-con" is up to you.) Following my curiosity, I have read countless books, scientific papers, and blog entries on the subject — as much as I could bear. At the same time, I was able to reflect my readings in real life, selling successfully in many environments — from city streets to boardrooms — and building several smaller businesses. Additionally, I have spent time being involved and serving on the board of some charitable organizations. Behavecon has helped me understand why many things I had tried worked or failed. Therefore, I could get better. And so can you!

---

[2] Schweinehund is a German word that literally translates to "swine hound." It refers to your lazy inner self that wants to do something but just can't get around to actually do it.

I am not Mr. Know-It-All. To the contrary, I have made and am still making mistakes. In the course of my life, I have always sought to learn as much as possible and to grow spiritually as well as financially. In this book, I share what helped me earn, save, and grow or what helped me understand why I failed and I lost so much in some cases.

In the end, I am like you. Eager to learn. In some directions I have advanced farther, whereas you have a leg up on me in many others.

How to Use This Book

Three sorts of people I find when I look around me every day: the constant, the convenient, and the innovators. The constant do as they always do. If you fall into this group, you probably picked up this book by mistake, so put it away. The convenient are aware that something is subpar and that change would be the right thing to do, so they pick up this and many other self-help books, read them, but do not change their habits. The third group is different in that they embrace change, progress, and innovation. They try new stuff and keep at it or make further changes if it does not yield the desired results. This book should be fun to read; its full benefits, however, you will only reap by employing the learnings and changing your actions, your habits, your life. This is a practical book inviting you to become an innovator.

Working with this book you can either read cover to cover as you learn about yourself and others. But I would not blame you if instead you chose to skip right to the parts most relevant to you. All I ask of you is that you read the final chapter, "Making It Happen," in its entirety. It will help you turn the ship around and become the lifestyle innovator you want to be.

As you go through the book, question yourself. They say, "Half of what we know is wrong. But we do not know which half it is." Before you read, ask, what do you want to learn from this book? While you are reading, challenge my teaching. Accept it when you find it is right. Engage in a discussion about anything you see different. Science is like a river. As countless gallons of water are flowing toward the shore, a new bed is formed — most of the time gradually, sometimes in impressive events, breaking century-old dams.

Don't let your skepticism serve as an excuse for not doing anything. If you are uncertain, try it. Take the current teaching as hypothesis. If you disprove it, share the new knowledge you gained and implement what you found. This is how simple the science of trial and error really is.

Finally, believe. Optimistic baseball batters hit the ball 20% more often than others under pressure. It is a tough world out there in the field, but you too can hit the ball! And hitting 20% more than the others will already catapult you to the top.[3]

Terminology

Producer, *seller*, *merchant*, and *vendor* are used synonymously. Also, *consumer*, *buyer*, *purchaser*, and

---

[3] According to Werner Mickler, psychologist at the German Soccer Federation, one strategy to become more optimistic is to relive moments of success and achievement, which you undoubtedly have, in your mind.

you are the same for the purpose of this work.

Because I lived in different countries with different currencies, some of the examples I use are in dollars and some are in euros. For the benefit of the international readers, I decided to leave them in their original currency, as they are applicable irrespective of the exact amounts anyway.

Key Points to Remember

- You want and deserve to get more out of your life!
- Financial riches are a means, not a goal in themselves.
- We are *irrational* in the ways we think and act. Therefore, we need to outsmart our subconscious in order not to be outsmarted by our economic environment.
- Get ready for some hard and rewarding work. Stay optimistic. You can do it.

This was just the introduction. Now, enjoy!

GROUND ZERO

In this part ...

The action starts. You begin to evaluate your life's status quo in depth. This book is not a one size fits all, but a toolbox for your to work with as applicable. After several easy to follow exercises you will know what you own and owe, what you earn and spend. Then, at the core of this section, we figure out what got you there and why - the underlying causes. This will be the ground zero for your new future. Lawn mowers and Japanese knives play a strong role as well as gambling and Versailles. Come, explore!

Your Assets

"I know what I do not know. To this day, I do not know
technology, and I do not know finance or accounting."
— Bernie Ebbers
Cofounder and former CEO of WorldCom (*Time* magazine named
him the 10th most corrupt CEO of all time.)

"Good order is the foundation of all things."
— Edmund Burke
18th-century Irish statesman

Which quote describes your situation most
adequately? It is time for a self-assessment. In this part
of the book, you will figure out what you own or owe
and what behaviors got you there. We are going to
turn what you have into the best foundation possible
so you will be ready to go with a vengeance.

Your Financial Assets and Liabilities

Take a sheet of paper or the spreadsheet from the
supporting material of this book. On the left, list all
financial assets and liabilities by name, such as cash,
checking accounts, money owed by friends or family,
401(k)s, IRAs, expected inheritances, credit cards, car
loans, mortgages, etc. Group them by duration and

add two subtotal lines. In the top line, you can put the years starting with the current one. Now fill in the cells for this year with the respective amounts. All amounts owed get a negative sign. At the very bottom, let us add a grand total line. This is your total net worth, and you can now monitor how it develops. Because you grouped the items by their duration, you can also calculate net worths with respect to certain time frames. If you are really excited about this, you could even go through your files and reconstruct the past years.

all data in USD	2013	2014	2015	Next Steps
Total Assets	**173.904**			Sample data provided is for illustration purposes only.
Cash and Liquid Assets (3 months or less)	**30.404**			Adding further time categories for the long term might be beneficial in some cases.
Cash	250			
Checking Accounts	3.254			
Savings Accounts	0			
Money Market Accounts	25.000			Find investment opportunities that yield more.
Short Running Receivables				
Family	1.000			
Friends	0			
Employer	400			
IRS	500			
Health Insurance	0			
Other	0			
Medium Term Investments (3 months - 3 years)	**3.500**			
Health Savings Account	2.000			
Lease Deposits	1.500			
Stock Portfolios	0			
Dedicated Savings Accounts	0			
Other	0			
Long Term Investments (more than 3 years)	**140.000**			Start building up an IRA plan as it is government sponsored.
401k	30.000			Make maximum contributions to IRA and/or 401(K) for a while and transfer these 10K to your
IRA	0			checking account to cover living expenses during that period.
Retirement Savings	10.000			
Investment Type Life Insurance	0			Don't be overly optimistic here, your parents might decide spending some or all of that money.
Expected Inheritances	100.000			
Other	0			

16

all data in USD	2013	2014	2015	Next Steps
Total Liabilities	**-461.112**			
Short Term Liabilities (3 months or less)	**-4.612**			
Credit Cards	-4.612			Immediately repay credit cards in full with checking and money market accounts.
Short Term Bank debt	0			
Short Running Payables				
Family	0			
Friends	0			
Employer	0			
IRS	0			
Other	0			
Medium Term Liabilities (3 months - 3 years)	**-6.500**			
Consumer Debt, Financed Purchases	-3.000			Immediately repay in full with money market accounts if possible without exaggerated fee.
Car Loans / Lease Obligations	-3.500			If car loan, immediately repay in full to save on interest if possible without exaggerated fee. If lease, wait for lease to expire and purchase next car by paying cash.
Other	0			
Long Term Liabilities (more than 3 years)	**-450.000**			
Student Loan	-50.000			Repay as much as you can still reasonably afford to without creating other problems.
Mortgages	-400.000			Evaluate your property and see how you can best cover this longterm responsibility.
Other	0			
Total Financial Net Worth	**-287.208**			In this example the individual is doing ok in the next three years and probably feels like having a lot of money.
Short Term Net Worth	25.792			
Medium Term Net Worth	22.792			
Long Term Net Worth	-287.208			Yet there might be an issue in the long term.

Looking ahead, you will have to find a practical way of staying aware of your current net worth at any time. As doing this whole exercise on a daily basis will be mostly tedious without revealing much news, I suggest an incremental approach. That means going through the main accounts on a monthly basis and revisiting slow-moving investment accounts only annually or after known major incidents such as a market crash. Additionally, you will want to keep any current spending in mind. This requires some training, but you will easily get there over time.

Now, have a look at your sheet.

Is your grand total, your net worth, positive or negative?

If there is any debt, are there any assets too? What is the ratio of debt to assets? Your lenders will want you to have many assets so they will feel comfortable that you can eventually pay them back. However, for you, having assets and debt means that by living closer to your net worth—i.e., with fewer assets and debt— you would pay less interest in some cases without even having to change anything in your daily life. Therefore, the action advice is clear: Pay off all your debt, or as much as you possibly can, starting with the highest-interest debt first.

As you do so, watch possible contract penalties from lenders for premature debt release. They might be so high that it is actually not worth paying up the debt early. In that case, try to negotiate.

If you have a troubled credit history, beware not to trouble it any more. After paying off your credit card debt, slowly start canceling cards at a rate of about one a quarter. Start with the most expensive ones and the ones with the worst or shortest history. This way, your FICO score will not take too much of a hit or might even improve. For more on FICO scores, read chapter 1 of *The Money Book for the Young, Fabulous & Broke* by Suze Orman.

What does your net worth look like in various time frames?

By looking at your short-term net worth in respect to your medium- and long-term net worth, you can see when you will run into financial trouble long before it happens. For example, you might have a lot of cash on hand today and feel pretty rich; however, huge mortgage payments might be looming just over the horizon. Or you might appear to be in total financial chaos today, but there is a silver lining as all troubles are only temporary. Find out more by looking at the bottom 3 indicators on your spreadsheet.

How many accounts with similar features are there?

For instance, do you have multiple checking accounts with different institutions? Reduce the number of accounts to save on fees and, more important, administration time. Administration is easily underestimated. Think of opening the account, reviewing the statements, receiving mail, troubleshooting, etc. Consider also that each account takes up mindshare for passwords and even time for your tax return.

Within one risk class, always put your money into the account with the highest return. So if you can find an interest-bearing, FDIC-insured, and free checking account, put all your checking money into it. For all your immediately accessible savings, you should look for the money market, savings account, or similar with the highest interest and no wait time for accessing funds.

What I said above regarding FICO scores applies to closing any type of account. So once again, you might want to consider what the optimal closing strategy is.

How much of your financial assets are in high-risk classes, such as stocks?

Stocks are amazing. They earn you bragging rights. You can lull your friends in with your amazing stock picks and news from the stock market. When you win, you always have an impressive story to tell; and when you lose, you could feel like a fallen hero, but you will come back! Unfortunately, individual stock investments are extremely high risk and neither a short- nor a long-term effective investment strategy for private investors.

In general, you will want to have most of your money in boring low-risk accounts. Have a look at *I Will Teach You to Be Rich* by Ramit Sethi for a consistently well-performing but low-sex-appeal investing strategy.

If you have historical data, what kind of development do you find?

Your Valuables

Up to now, we have only looked at your financial assets, but there is more. What about all the physical things you own?

Take another sheet of paper (or the spreadsheet from the supporting material) and inventory all valuables above a certain threshold of current estimated market value. That threshold should be an amount that you consider substantial. For a student, $5 might be substantial; for a lawyer, $50 or even $150 might be that number. Ideally, it will be your hourly income as discussed in the next chapter. Items considered as valuables in the sense of this chapter are everything material you own—for example, stereos, cameras, silverware, collector's items, vases, furniture, and your car. Don't forget what you have in your garage or at your parents' house. For purposes of simplification, you can group identical items—for instance, four dining room chairs. Maybe you once created a similar list when purchasing a homeowner's or renter's insurance. Once you are done, rank it by the frequency of use: daily use (e.g., dishes), weekly use (e.g., vacuum cleaner), monthly use (e.g., boat), annual use (e.g., garden furniture), even less frequent use (e.g., power sledgehammer), never used (e.g., that gold-colored orb Aunt Mary gave you 12 years ago).

	Current Market Value	Special Value Item (Y/N)	Usage Frequency	
				This list contains a lot of items, as you fill it in, you may skip irrelevant ones. For example pots/pans might not constitute enough value in your case, so leave them out.
				Add additional items as you see fit.
Living Room/Family Room				
carpet/rugs				
curtains/drapes				
sofa				
coffee table				
bookcase				
chairs				
pictures/wall hangings				
desks				
clocks				
lamps				
television				
set-top boxes, e.g. AppleTV				
camcorder				
CD/DVD player				
stereo				
radio				
speakers				
records/tapes/CDs/ DVDs				
piano/musical instrument				
fireplace equipment				
plants/planters				
vases				
mirrors				
... (to be continued in supporting material)				

Our subconscious offers a couple of trip wires for determining the fair market value. We prize what we have more than what we do not. In an experiment to illustrate this conducted at the Duke University campus, students were offered tickets to an important ball game. It turned out that, on average, they were willing to fork over $166 for a ticket to the game. A control group that had been assigned tickets before would not sell for less than $2,411. Ownership triggers emotions, and we want to be compensated disproportionally. This is the *ownership bias* or *endowment effect* as it is called by Richard Thaler.

Add the *illusion of control* as indicated by the fact that people will sell a handpicked lottery ticket with their numbers only for at least for four times its original price. It is evident that the lottery probabilities remain unaffected from you purchasing the ticket. However, it is much less evident that the likeliness to appreciate in value of a stock or mutual fund you bought does not change, especially as your subconscious believes exactly that.

Therefore, you will want to ask yourself, first of all, "How much would I pay for this if I would not have it in my possession?" Look just at the physical item. Any history is irrelevant. You might have inherited that watch from your grandfather, and thus it is of special value to you. Almost certainly, you would pay anything to get it back, but that is not the point here. Imagine all you could buy is a watch that looks alike but is of unknown history.

Only as a second step, consider how much you would want to get for it. When you note the market value, use the value you determined with the first question. If the value you place on the item is considerably higher, make note in the special value column.

Ever published your personal *Sears Catalog*? You are about to. From my experience, it takes you about one hour to sell something through eBay or a similar outlet, including the time to package and ship the goods. Therefore, anything is a great deal for increasing your net worth that

(1) you do not need,

(2) you can sell within one hour, and

(3) fetches more than you could otherwise earn during that hour.

Additionally, if you invest that money, you can earn a return, which is much better than a deteriorating stereo set in your basement.

Next step: Anything you want to get rid of that is worth less than one hour, you can either sell in bundles, offer at a garage sale or flea market, donate to charity and claim a tax deduction, or simply toss out. When claiming charity donations, watch out for the annual limits and spread your donations over a period of time if necessary. A good trick is to spread donations into boxes for the years to come and donate the boxes as time goes by without ever opening them again. If you look at the content once more, a feeling of *loss aversion* will strike you and reduce your willingness to part.

It feels tough, but once you get rid of something, it is a delight! So focus not on giving up but on the freedom you could attain. What exactly is unnecessary? Start with the items you use the least and progress on your list toward the most frequently used items. Then determine if their function could be accomplished without them or by a cheaper means. This could be based on something you already have or you could purchase with the proceeds from the item's sale while still pocketing a substantial difference. Also, a rarely required item could be replaced by a service provider delivering the function instead of you actually owning the tools required to perform it yourself. A few examples:

1. I do not have an ironing board and an iron.

My shirts go to the dry cleaner, and everything else is wrinkle free. If once in a blue moon I need one, I ask my neighbor.

Moreover, I do not have a vacuum cleaner anymore because I ask my cleaning lady to bring hers. That saves space and money, and I never need to spend time to buy a cleaner or vacuum bags. Please note: I do not have a carpet, so I can help myself with a broom in case of a mishap.

2. How many lawn mowers could you possibly need in one subsection?

Why not buy one together with a few neighbors? Or simply rent one occasionally? I know this is not easy. I had to work on my parents for quite a while until they were ready to ask their neighbors to build a joint driveway instead of both parties having the narrowest trail you can imagine. Guess how many scratched doors and fenders we have had in the driveway since. None! And before? Confidential. It is the greatest invention since sliced bread.

There is more and more of these consumer-to-consumer swap sites going online. You can use those, but the old-fashioned way of asking your neighbors is oftentimes just as rewarding, if not more.

3. In my kitchen, I have an extremely sharp Japanese knife.

When I was a teenager, my mom took me to see Kevin Costner and Whitney Houston in *The Bodyguard*.

The only scene I remember is Kevin's intense training session with his samurai sword. As Whitney rolls in, part of their tense flirting is her holding his sword steady pointed at him. He gallantly pulls her scarf and throws it into the air. "Watch this." As it sails down to the floor, it passes the sword, which effortlessly separates it into two halves. Mystical. I could not possibly imagine anything so sharp as to cut a silk scarf under nothing but the pressure of its own weight.

Introducing my Japanese kitchen knife. It is the most expensive tool. And when I say sharp, I am talking about a degree of sharpness that goes beyond anything you have ever experienced from the sharpest supermarket kitchen knife or even premium German or American knife. Granted, working with such a knife takes some practice — and bloodshed — but it makes all sorts of kitchen aids obsolete. I can cut an onion faster, cleaner, and into smaller pieces than any onion cutter. If I consider the time it takes to clean the knife versus the onion cutter, I am already preparing deserts when in the past I was still rinsing the onion cutter. While the knife was expensive, it will probably last forever, as it does not have any moving parts.

Especially if you are not a large family but single or a couple, most of the advances in household tools as sold on shopping TV channels really don't offer that much of value once you carefully consider it.

Selling unnecessary items can be highly rewarding and relieving in a financial as well as psychological sense. It might even be sensible to cut down the hours at work temporarily and spend the time selling those items if you can absolutely not fit this into your free time.

BEHAVECON

Finally, with all the money you have just earned in this chapter, pay off more debt, if there is still any left.

Side Note on Driving and Riding Value Cycles

Not all market values remain constant or decline over time. Your clothes and fashion items exhibit a cyclical market value. Some items might become a classic once vintage. So keep your old designer clothes or that first-generation iPhone if you have free storage and don't move too often.

After storing clothes for 20 years, they will be hip again. But there is a caveat: The clothes and especially you need to stay in shape over time. Otherwise, you will have to sell them 20 years down the road. What an incentive! Spend less and live longer. :)

The iPhone 1 is already fetching prices higher than the current model in some instances. And it has only been five years since it was launched.

To fetch the highest sales price, keep the original packaging. Your customer will pay for the pleasure of unboxing a seemingly newer item. But remember to discard it once the item itself is broken or otherwise not fit for sale anymore.

When determining your offer price, as mentioned above, start with a fair price without expecting the buyer to share your emotional bonds. Then put a reasonable charge on top so there is some room to negotiate.

Built on Escalating Commitment

Above, you have taken stock and implemented a few quick fixes. Maybe you are wondering, how did I get here in life?

The sum of your past decisions and actions has led you to this point. And there were a lot of tiny ones accumulating to the grand scheme that is your life today. On the way, you have done good and bad things. I assume you have picked up this book as you want to be better. Improving means change. And that also means implicitly admitting that things we did in the past were not ideal. Oftentimes, that feels very difficult. A psychological phenomenon called *escalating commitment* prevents us from doing so.

It works like this: Once we have taken a position or decided on a course of action, we start to defend it and look for reasons why it is right. This is called *confirmation bias*. Based on this, we start investing ourselves further into it. The ensuing spiral is the escalating commitment. This might be a small thing such as haphazardly growing a beard. On day 1, you forget to shave. On day 2, you stand in front of the mirror and you think, *Oh, it doesn't look that bad.* And you skip it again in favor of spending a few more minutes reading the morning paper. The next day, you are like, *Well, one more day won't make a difference.* Without shaving, you leave the house. And thereafter, you don't even question the new morning ritual until someone at work approaches you and asks whether you are growing a beard. Only then you realize the fundamental change in your appearance.

The same principle can explain large public construction "bonanzas" such as the Shoreham

Nuclear Power Plant in Long Island, New York, which was never opened after 23 years of extended construction. Apparently, nobody ever asked if they were still on the right track, so they all just kept going.

It is one of the root causes of the recent financial crisis, where we kept on taking out mortgages on our homes because it felt right. After all, we just did a little more of what we had been doing all along. This is why change is so difficult, even if we know it is for the better.

Above, I have used negative examples to illustrate escalating commitment. Yet it works just as well to your benefit. If your goal is to exercise every day before breakfast, it will only be tough in the beginning. After a few days, you will not consciously make the decision anymore. It just happens.

So what you really need is a key to break the vicious cycles you are already in. I invite you to question your past decisions, your ongoing habits, the projects you are currently involved in. Everything we do is prone to this phenomenon. Therefore, may the "why" be your new best friend. Step back and reevaluate regularly. It does not matter how much you have spent in money, time, or thought. These are sunk costs. They are all irrevocably gone. It only matters what the future prospects are. Yes, you can lose your face by pulling out of something you have strongly supported before. People might even perceive you as erratic. But would you rather be considered a Steve Jobs and win big, or a consistent failure?

Attracting and Repelling Money

You should have a clear picture of your assets by now. One of the key assets is money as it enables you do many great things.

Although money will seem quite real to you, it is just a belief, a very strong idea of sorts. Here is a little story. Paris of the South—Buenos Aires, December 2011. I was on a cab ride home after I had taken a stroll through the busy streets. When paying, the cab driver gave me some change, which I unsuspiciously put into my wallet. Later at a post office, I wanted to buy some stamps for postcards to send home. Trying to pay with the bills I received from the cabbie, I was dumbfounded when told that one of them was a fake. The clerk happily returned it to me, openly suggesting to spend it elsewhere. At a polo tournament sports event the next day, it was accepted without complaint.

Money is just a belief. It works as long as both parties deeply accept that. Therefore, it is absolutely essential that you have a positive attitude about money. The *law of attraction* is widely promoted by the book *The Secret*. Typically, money evokes rather pointed associations. We either hate it or love it. The law of attraction states that if we love money and deal with it in enjoyment, it will flow freely to us. While this law is far from scientifically proven, there is a certain causality in my experience that can be described as a *law of repulsion*.

If you hate someone, you do not want to spend time with that person. If in turn you are forced to do so, you do it with resistance; you try to think about other things on your mind, and you do not even give that individual the chance to make a positive impression on you. Whether you like it or not, that is the behavior your subconscious leads you into. The same applies to money. If you despise it, you do not spend time pondering your financial situation and the impact certain activities have on it.

No matter how you feel about it, money is the lifeblood of our economy. We are exposed to it every day and in many forms. Almost everything we do revolves in one way or the other around money. There is no way to evade it. Even Hanna Poddig, a German woman who refuses to work and only lives from things given to her or taken from dumpsters, still exists in a world of money. She does not touch the cash, but it is others that buy stuff for her. No matter how you spin it, money is the game. By understanding and embracing this actively, you can enter the game and play. Playing means investing yourself and some of your time, thoughts, and effort into it with a positive attitude. You too can win in this game if you truly want to.

Hate money and associate it with trouble, and you will always subconsciously avoid it and thus not have it. But on falling for money, I also want to caution you to a certain extent: While to love is to spend money confidently and to attract it, greed is to freeze in fear of its loss and to put it above other higher values. Money should be a positive idea in your mind, not an all-encompassing overwhelming, ravenous hunger that clouds your judgment. It is only a means to an end.

The Accounts in Your Mind

While today almost everyone has a bank account, people have always had mental accounts as well. It has been found that we keep certain accounts for various areas of life and label resources and consumption accordingly. Money in those accounts, we treat very differently, even though, rationally, it is all the same money with identical value. Money is fungible, but most of the time, we don't treat it that way, thereby effectively devaluing it. Here are a few examples from literature.

A couple goes to a fishing trip and sends a large amount of salmon back home. Unfortunately, the package gets lost, but they get a $300 compensation. After they return home, they go for the most expensive dinner of their life and spend $225 (in 1985, yummy). What happened here is that they saw the $300 as a windfall profit; they would certainly not have eaten that dinner if they had each received a $150 net pay raise, even though in the long term that would have yielded them more riches. In effect, mental accounting made them spend more money than they rationally wanted and than was necessary.

Two guys are at a poker table; one is up $50 in the game, and the other one is still even but he has a $50 gain realized by selling some stock earlier that day. The first one has a queen-high flush and calls a $10 bet. The second one folds despite having a king-high flush. After the first one wins, the second player thinks that he would have called too if he had been $50 up. Here, being ahead in the game induces more risk-prone behavior, but he does not take his entire financial position into account, which he reasonably should have done.

The above described effect is not primarily based on the emotional charge of the situation. Instead, we generally tend to group income into accounts for regular income and windfall. Also, we group expenses into necessary consumption and hedonistic spending. Then we typically prefer to spend our windfall on hedonistic endeavors. Furthermore, it turns out that we are more inclined to spend money for hedonistic purposes if it comes out of our checking account than if it comes out of a savings account. This is not a carefully weighted rational decision. It is hardwired into our brains, and we do so without thinking.

So if you see yourself always out of cash before your next paycheck, open a savings account and automatically transfer a good portion (twice as much as you initially thought you could) of your paycheck in there. Only then start allocating the remainder for your ongoing expenses. And if you earn some unexpected income, remember this fallacy and allow yourself only to celebrate a small portion of it, saving the rest for later.

Another issue is how often we balance our mental accounts. If we balance on a weekly basis, we are less likely to spend last week's lottery win on a fancy skiing trip this week; but if we consolidate on a monthly basis, we are happy to do so.

Our willingness to spend money varies among mental accounts. This indicates that we apply different reasoning in the decision making process for each of them. Consumption of daily necessities happens without much reasoning, whereas we have to explain luxurious purchases to ourselves because they might violate certain principles we cherish. So we tend to fall for opportunities once our mental account for hedonistic purposes is filled. Also oftentimes we choose the most defensible rather than the best option. We cannot do without a living room sofa, but certainly without an extravagant 18th-century canopy bed, or so we think. This effect is called *reason-based choice*. You will want to extend this to each individual decision and not just to your main mental accounts. Of course, life can get very different if you start evaluating every grocery item you buy like this, but once you do this for a while, you will start building new habits and new mental accounts that will be more favorable to your purposes. Then a year later, you can revisit.

Finally, to show how counterintuitive mental accounting can get, one last example by Nobel laureate Daniel Kahneman: Imagine you are going to the movies. At the box office, you realize that you have lost the $10 bill that you had seen in your wallet earlier that day. What do you do? Chances are you will still buy a ticket worth $10 and enjoy the movie. Now imagine a different scenario where you had purchased the $10 ticket in advance and at the box office you notice that you have lost the said ticket. What do you do? Would you buy a new one? Apparently, people are now more likely to call it a day and go home. Paying twice for the same show is out of the question to them, whereas the lost $10 dollar bill was presumably just charged to their general revenue/loss account.

The limits imposed by mental accounting can be mitigated by knowing your total net worth at every instant and by looking at expenses with respect to that.

This way, you can maintain a comprehensive view of the outcomes. There is no need to keep all the mental accounts in the black at all times as long as your total net worth is going into the desired direction.

Why We Carry Debt

Whether you found some debt on your spreadsheet or just for your future protection, here is an elaboration of the root causes for indebtedness:

It is plain *simple*. An urge to purchase something is easily fulfilled with a credit card. There is no worrying, whether we actually have the money. The credit is granted immediately, without further questioning.

We are *procrastinators*. Just as we did not do our homework until the eleventh hour in high school, we gladly accept the prospect of getting the merchandise today and paying as late as possible.

We are confident, we are great, and who could deny us any wish? We are the princes and princesses of this world, and if we see something, we have a right to it. We have a right to the new iPad, a right to a Cadillac. I want, I take, I pay—later. In short, the feeling of *entitlement* is a psychological phenomenon of our understanding that we deserve. And debt not only makes it possible for us to fulfill those desires but also, by fulfilling, reinforces this behavior as we teach our subconscious that we were indeed entitled.

We have come to expect a lot from the life of *instant gratification*. Our parents pampered us so much by granting every wish immediately without us having to wonder about the consequences. Amazon.com taught us next-day delivery on a large scale. This instant gratification goes hand in hand with entitlement as it tightens the feedback loop between desire and gratification even more.

The flip side of instant gratification is pain. Our desire can become so strong that we experience it as more painful than obtaining the object while incurring debt. When this happens, we usually stop rationalizing and simply give in.

Imagine a couple having saved $150,000 toward their dream vacation property. They earn 4% on their investment. Also, they have just bought a new car for $40,000, and they financed that at 10%. As a matter of fact, the couple is wasting a lot of money by not just taking the money for the car out of their savings account. This happens because they subtly believe that they might not repay themselves, but they are sure to repay the bank as the bank will collect. They perform the above-described *mental accounting*. However, I have seen this in many cases where I would attribute it more to ignorance or a simple wish of having a large savings account.

Having the desire to have some *emergency cash on hand* is another form of mental accounting that declines the idea of total net worth. While the desire is understandable, a credit card or a line of credit on your checking account can serve this purpose much better. That way, you will only pay interest if you actually run into that emergency. Per definition, an emergency is nothing that happens regularly. Therefore, you should not be paying much interest. You only want to have emergency cash on hand if you do not have any debt.

"It was *inevitable*. There was no other way. It was an emergency. We really needed something." Really? In most cases, this should raise a red flag as it is in truth only a camouflage version of one of the above.

We took on some *good debt*. Some forms of debt are actually justifiable. It is all the cases where the return on the money borrowed exceeds the interest paid. Sometimes this works because what you do with the money is so smart. Sometimes it works because the interest gets tax-exempt. However, most of the time, this does *not* work and you are just buying something that you simply cannot afford, or the return on your financed investment is unexpectedly lower than the interest you need to pay. In this case, you pay interest on something that you could not afford in the first place, and thus it gets even more expensive. In turn, you can afford even fewer other things, which you could otherwise have easily afforded.

Key Points to Remember

- You now have a clear understanding of your *financial assets* and *liabilities*. You also know your *valuables* and how often you use them. If not, go back and fill in the spreadsheet now.
- You have cleaned up your financials and sold off unnecessary items or at least scheduled some time in the near future to do so.
- *Ownership bias*: We prize what we have more than what we have not. Try to evaluate decisions from both perspectives.
- *Illusion of control*: We believe in better odds if we are involved in the process, even though it is still fully random. (Think picking lottery numbers or stocks.) So don't bother spending time involving yourself in random processes.
- *Escalating commitment*: *Confirmation bias* makes us seek reasons to confirm that what we have just done was right. Subsequently, doing more of it and seeking even more confirmation is called escalating commitment. It can create vicious circles or positive reinforcement loops.
- *Law of repulsion*: Our subconscious wants to protect us. It will go to great lengths to ensure we don't get what we don't want. Therefore, embrace money! It is the lifeblood of our economy, and even though you might be convinced that the world would be better off without it, it is here to stay, and your quality of life depends on it. Everything else is utopia.

- *Mental accounting.* We allocate our money to mental accounts earmarked for specific purposes and spend it accordingly. Inefficient allocation can create unnecessary financial burdens.

- *Reason-based choice*: Carefully and consciously evaluating a decision seeking the best option rather than the best defensible or easiest one. Do it as much as possible, especially when the stakes are high.

- Always know your *financial net worth*.

- Seven out of eight reasons for *debt* are reasons not good enough to take on debt. Spend only the money you have.

Your Income and Spending of Money and Time

"Time is more valuable than money. You can get more money,
but you cannot get more time."
—Jim Rohn
Late American entrepreneur, author, and motivational speaker

"Money is only a tool. It will take you wherever you wish, but
it will not replace you as the driver."
— Ayn Rand
20th-century Russian-American novelist, philosopher, playwright,
and screenwriter

Do you live in Denver? If so, you might have participated in a study of local shoppers. It indicated that families making more than \$70K/year pay 5% more for the same set of goods than families making less than \$30K. OK, they can afford it, you might say. Singles without children pay 10% less across the board than families with five members or more. Families with a head of the family in the early 40s pay 8% more than those with one in the early 20s or 60s. Is that fair? Why should those that need it more get punished? In part, this is because of the differences in how we value time and money. A soccer mom doesn't have the time to figure out the cheapest store; she will simply go to the most convenient one, won't she? It's also because it's much easier to fool someone who has other stuff on her mind. So we have to find ways to concentrate very efficiently, without taking too much attention away from other parts of our life.

Peter Drucker coined the expression "What gets measured gets managed." Let's measure! Collect all recurring income and spending. This will be the most tedious task of this book as you will have to go through your credit card and checking account statements of the entire past year to ensure completeness. Take the last 12 months. Before you are done, check if you missed anything. Maybe you have paid your car insurance a little early in one year, so it was not in the year you analyzed, or it was in there twice. You might be thinking that all this is too much work, or you might not see any possible benefits as you only have very little income and expenses anyway. Take a leap of faith. Do it.

On a side note, I have personally done this for several years with each and every expense, not just the recurring ones, and it really helped me to see where my money was going. Also simply knowing that you will have to get a receipt and log it somewhere will reduce your eagerness to spend as we are all lazy. So if you want to go a step farther, feel free to join me. And if going backward is too painful, just do it moving forward as you go. Not having your statements anymore is no excuse.

As you create your list, first, start with all incomes, such as work income, royalty income, Google Ads income from your blog, interest income, rent income if you have any properties, and income from other sources, e.g., from parents, alimonies, or gifts. Don't worry if you don't have all these sources, yet. Then continue with the recurring payments you have, such as insurances, retirement, housing related (rent, utilities, etc.), car, lotteries, memberships, debt service (interest and repayment of the principal), communication, bank fees, fun stuff, e.g., magazine subscriptions.

	2013	2014	2015
Income	0		
Work			
Financial (Interest, Dividends)			
Royalties			
Real estate			
Online activities			
Parental support			
Alimonies			
Stipends			
Gifts			
...			
Spending	0		
Taxes			
Housing	0		
Place			
Communications			
Cable/TV			
Utilities			
...			
Mobility	0		
Vehicles			
Gas			
Maintenance			

	2013	2014	2015
Public transport			
...			
Financial	0		
Insurances			
Bank fees			
Debt service			
Lotteries			
Savings			
...			
Food	0		
Basic items			
Luxury food			
Alcoholic beverages			
Dining out			
...			
Entertainment	0		
Magazine subscriptions			
Event tickets			
Leisure travel			
Books			
Movie rental			
Cigarettes			
...			
Physical Performance /Appearance	0		
Medical / Dental / Visual			
Clothing			
Fitness club			
Hairdresser			
...			
Personal Development	0		
Books/media			
Classes			
...			

	2013	2014	2015
Miscellaneous	0		
Memberships			
Gifts			
Alimonies			
...			

The income section shows that you already make a lot of money. If it does not feel that way, this is because it goes out as fast as it comes in. Before we look at some specific behaviorally influenced improvement potentials, let's find out about your value of time as well.

Your One-Hour Rule

"Time is money." Isn't there more complexity to life? How can we get a link between time and money?

A janitor making $11 values an opportunity to make an additional $20 in one hour very differently than a lawyer making $500 an hour. While the lawyer would rather want to spend the hour doing something for herself, the janitor would probably prefer to work and get the cash. How about you?

In an average work year, there are about 2,000 hours. Thus, about 0.05% of your annual after-tax compensation is what you make during one hour. If you make $20K after tax, that means your *hourly income* is $10; if you make $100K after tax, it is $50. Not so fast. Into your calculations you also have to include the commute time as well as any time you work at home after hours. You want this to be a fair picture.

Do you work multiple jobs, or are you spending some time investing money that you already have or dealing with a property you own? If so, for your calculation, please use the overall hours you work in all those undertakings, and also take the overall income from all of them into one combined ratio. Then calculate the one-hour rule for each one individually. Now that you know your return on certain activities, try to shift your time to the job that provides the most return on your invested time. This way, without making less, you can free time to read or do whatever you like for a happier life.

Additionally, before shifting time allocations, you might want to reassess what the true value is that you create during those hours. Maybe you are not paid corresponding to the value that you create at one of your jobs. And that is something to discuss with your boss. Be confident about your contribution! You might also come to the conclusion that you are in an investment period in one of your activities with an expected payout period coming later. In that case, it might make sense to keep investing and making less today in return for future prospects.

Keep the figure for your total hourly income in mind so you can assess how long you need to work in order to be able to afford certain things.

So what is the value of your time? Is what we just calculated always the value of your time? The caveat with all those calculations is that they look very precise because they are mathematically derived, but still they are only a weak heuristic. Sometimes time is priceless—for instance, time with your kid or an aging parent. You will never get it back in the future. Some moments are instants in time that will live on in our memories if we choose to seize them or be gone forever if we decide otherwise.

Say you calculated your hour to be worth $15 or even $50. For $15, you can go to the movies; for $50, you can buy a day ticket to a ski resort. Find a number of things you can get for an hour's worth of work in terms of a pleasurable experience. Next time you are offered a carrot cake dessert for $8, remember that this is more than half an hour of work, more than half a ticket to the movies, or about as much as 50 minutes of music on iTunes. Then decide how much you crave it.

In general, the value of our time rises with age as we proceed in our careers, gain expertise and seniority, and then declines again before it rises once more. It has been found that time is most sacred around age 45, when wages and responsibilities peak and kids live at home. Once the kids move out, we seem to have substantially more time again. However, as we get older, it is not only the question of how much we could be making during that hour. It becomes more and more a question of how many hours remain and how much money you will still be able to spend. An 80-year-old lawyer with a rock-solid bank account really does not get much out of making another $500. Spending time with her children and grandchildren can be much more meaningful. This is a limitation to this model you ought to consider.

As a rule of thumb, you can remember that younger people tend to considerably overestimate the value of time, whereas older people tend to overestimate the value of money.

Money-Rich Time-Poor at a 100K?

How would you feel with 100K in cash? Let me be frank. It doesn't make you rich even though it might feel that way once you get there for the first time. I have spoken to quite a few individuals who have made it. And most of them concurred. While to a poor man 100K seems an awful lot of cash, once you have 100K consistently, you worry about not losing them, about how to invest them well and how to get to 1 million. And really, you cannot afford too many fancy things with them either. Lamborghini? No. Sailing yacht? No. I will give you a dream vacation, but that will already deplete 10–20K or more, depending on the scale of your dreams. There is not nearly as much lasting joy in having $100K as you might think. You will believe me when you get there.

Nonetheless, initially at that point, you might lean back, satisfied, and think that time is worth a lot more than money by then. As a matter of fact, time is still less important than many of us think at that point. As soon as you value time too much for its own sake, you will keep yourself from doing anything financially meaningful with it.

In my opinion, there is only one way out of the time-versus-money conundrum. Find projects that are fun and make money. As soon as spending time is not a cost to you anymore but actually a benefit, you earn twice. You make the money and get the enjoyment. As Arnold Schwarzenegger in his autobiography says, "Everything I did could have been my hobby. It *was* my hobby, in a way. I was passionate about all of it. My definition of living is to have excitement always; [...] Therefore, I seldom saw my life as hectic. The thought rarely even crossed my mind." And as someone who came to America with nothing but his body and succeeded in building a new industry, creating a real estate empire, becoming one of the world's most famous actors, and ultimately becoming governor of the State of California, he certainly had enough things to do every day. So if you feel like you are spending your time without satisfying return, consider Steve Jobs in his famous Stanford commencement address: "I have looked in the mirror every morning and asked myself: 'If today were the last day of my life, would I want to do what I am about to do today?' And whenever the answer has been 'No' for too many days in a row, I know I need to change something."

Protection

The big-ticket saving opportunity will most likely be all the insurances you have taken out. They are so prevalent because of our *loss aversion*. This refers to the fact that we care much more about preventing losses than acquiring gains. The more we have, the more worried we get and the more we freeze ourselves into protecting it instead of looking toward what can still be attained. This is so deeply rooted within our genome that it can even be found in monkeys. Really, successful people worry less about protecting what they have and spend more time focusing on making more. No matter if you are male or female, when someone invokes motives of self-protection, loss aversion increases, and we try to protect what we have.

Stuck in the Middle Class

Have a look at the only charts in the book below. Let me explain in detail. In A1, you can see the allocation of time depending on the perceived net worth of an individual. Looking at the $-axis, on the left you have little money, which symbolizes the beginning of your career, and at the far right, you are superrich. The t-axis represents how you allocate your time. The continuous line in the chart shows how much time is spent making money, and the dotted line indicates how much time is used protecting money or worrying about losing it. The sum of those two is always the same because you cannot change the hours in a day.

In A1, the two lines intersect to form what we call an *equilibrium*. In economics, an equilibrium is a state that is stable by itself, and a system will always move toward the equilibrium if otherwise left alone. You could also call it a trap. Whenever you get a little richer than the equilibrium, you start spending more time protecting that new wealth. Eventually, you lose some money again; and as you don't spend time on making more money, you cannot compensate for that loss. Before you know it, you are back at the equilibrium.

You can see the consequence of the equilibrium in A2, which shows the development of total net worth over time. Eventually, the net worth levels and does not increase anymore. You are stuck.

A1:

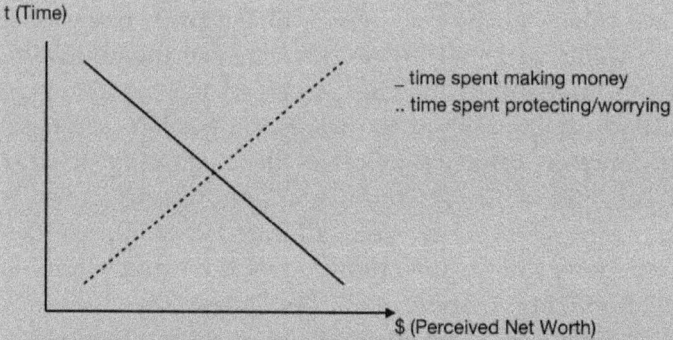

A2:

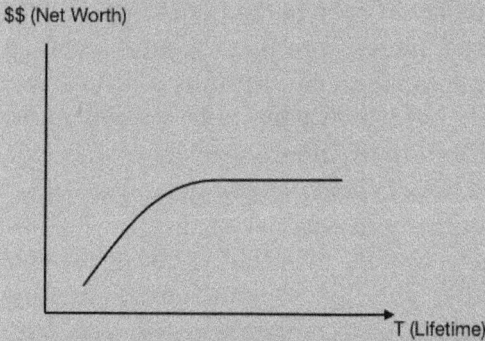

Leaving that equilibrium requires a deliberate effort. This is especially hard as it is a different type of effort than the one you needed initially to get to the equilibrium point.

What you want is to change your time allocation to a scenario like the one shown in B1 below. One way of doing so is to continuously fool yourself into believing that you don't own much. As you can see, in B1 we do not worry about protecting money, only about making more. The result is evident in B2, where our net worth keeps rising. The sky is the limit.

It is your choice in which of those worlds to live.

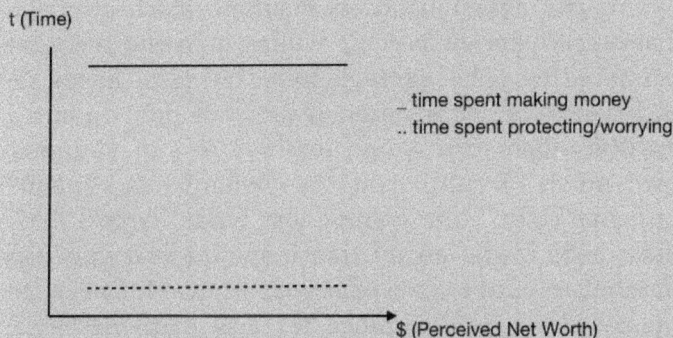

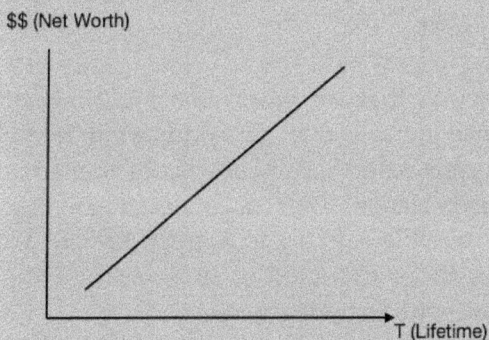

Now, start with canceling or reducing those insurances smartly. It will feel tough because on top of being loss averse, we are *risk averse*.

However, at this point in the book, you are already so much better off than before. Your overall risk is so much lower now that reducing insurance is the right thing to do. Your stronger foundation serves in part as insurance and can thus shield you from losing money every month on insurance premiums.

This risk aversion makes insurance such a terrific business. We are on average willing to spend more on insurance than the average loss. We hate losses as much as we cherish winning. If someone put you into a situation where you would lose $63 in 1 of 12 times, how much would you be willing to spend? Mathematically, your average loss would be $63 / 12, which is $5.25. So an insurance should cost you less than that amount to be worth your while. However, do not expect to get insurance for less than $10. That means that in 11 of 12 cases, the insurance company makes $10 and pays out $63 in 1 of 12. On average, they make $4.85. Not a bad deal, huh? Your risk aversion is their profit.

Another fallacy is that we worry too much about the potential consequences than the odds of it really happening. Everyone knows someone or of someone with a terrible experience. That does not mean that anything equally terrible is likely to happen to you. To the contrary, it is to be expected to find some of the worst fates among your acquaintances.

The theory of six degrees of separation states that, on average, we are connected to everyone on this planet in six steps. For example, you know Jennifer, Jennifer knows me, I know Marc, and Marc knows an aide in the White House, who in turn knows the president. According to this principle, you have probably heard of someone who was hurt in a flood, died in a car accident or fire, had his laptop stolen, broke his arm skiing, and so on.

That is just the average. The more people you know, the more appalling incidents you have heard of. At the time of this writing, I had about 7 million

second-degree contacts on LinkedIn and XING. Here are a few odds, and you can look for more online:
- Being killed by lightning: 1 in 2,320,000
- Chance of dying in an airplane accident: 1 in 354,319
- Odds of being murdered: 1 in 18,000

And really, I know people or of people with all these fates, and yet I still walk around in downtown Chicago occasionally at 4:00 a.m., jog in the rain, and fly a lot.

Our fear is further stirred by media reports that tell the stories of people in the far corners of the world. Media loves emotional stories like surfers with shark bites or anacondas feasting on wildlife tourists. On top of that, it is an insurance agent's business to tell us about all the remote cases where something has happened. Good and bad things occur — whether you know about it or not does not change the probability of you experiencing it. However, *selective perception* makes our subconscious open the filters for whatever we have indicated to have an interest in. This might be accidents of a certain type after an insurance broker has told us about them. Suddenly, we find them all around us and start feeling like we are a disaster waiting to happen, when really all there is, is a huge business waiting to happen.

A true but somewhat unfortunate point of view is that if a company wants to insure you, they believe the odds are in their favor. If they do not want to insure you, that is when you should consider getting insurance. Back to our example above, where the insurance made $4.85. That is the risk premium you pay for getting rid of the risk. An insurance provider will never offer you a deal where you win on average — they just can't. If they did, they would go out of business. Knowing that it is clear that you should have as little insurance as possible. Insurances are there to help in cases of life-threatening emergencies, i.e., for situations that you could not get out of without them anymore. Nothing else. Furthermore, insuring against the things that happen anyway is not insurance but an expensive way of financing. There are better ways.

Therefore, my car insurance has the highest deductible you can image. When I shopped for it, I realized that a $500 increase in the deductible saves me about $250 in premiums in the first year. If I get into an accident fewer than once every two years, I am making money. And in the last ten years of driving, I have certainly exceeded that average. You can even go as far as to say that since you could afford a new car anyway, you simply skip collision insurance altogether.

There are really only two points related to your car where you need protection. First, if you should get into a liability issue, you could be in serious financial trouble. Second, if you are hurt in a serious traffic accident, you will need all sorts of treatments. Dramatic brain injuries, among other things, can significantly impact your life in the short and long term, and someone will have to cover all the treatment cost plus your foregone income.

In cases like the above, you will be glad to have some disability insurance, unless you are wealthy enough already. As there are many types of disability insurance, the choice is not easy. Personally, I have purchased one, and it is very basic and cheap. It only pays if I literally cannot do anything anymore. My philosophy is that if I cannot write anymore, I will just do something else. That's life. I am certainly not willing to pay a hefty premium every month for the remote prospect of being unable to write one day. But this one is really a question of how far you feel comfortable in going.

Health insurance is similar to your automotive coverage. Usually, a high deductible will be a good thing. If you stay healthy, you will save the money. If you do not, you pay your deductible, but usually your monthly rates are so much lower that you are still better off. Another way of cutting down on insurance is available for homeowner's or renter's insurance. Instead of buying expensive insurance, you can simply put your valuable jewelry in a bank safe deposit box. That will already be insured and comes at a negligible annual fee compared to the adder your policy would charge. Of course, this won't work for your Monet on the wall.

Once you have left what you really need, shop around. No company is obliged to offer you a good deal; you are obliged to choose the company with the best deal. While doing that, see if you can consolidate. Carriers usually offer discounts if you have multiple insurances. Also check for discounts through American Express, alumni associations, unions, etc. See if you can get a better rate if your spouse or parent takes out the insurance in their name instead.

Your Bank

Banking dates back to the first days of civilization. As soon as money was invented, there was a need for it to be available everywhere. The bank's role was to provide it wherever it was needed. Too bad every fiefdom minted its own currency. So one of the initial forms of banking was currency exchange, as referred to in the narrative of Jesus cleansing the temple in Jerusalem 2,000 years ago. Eventually, more than a thousand years later, the Knights Templar — originally a pious military order bound to poverty by oath — offered the vastest banking network spanning Europe and parts of the Middle East. Their culminating power was also their eventual downfall. Banks throughout history that started out with humble goals had oftentimes become so powerful to effectively rule governments.

Fast-forward to today. By March 28, 2012, the Congressional Budget Office (CBO) estimated total disbursements would be $431 billion for the Troubled Assets Relief Program (TARP), the basic bank bailout package for the 2008 crisis. Effectively this is a transfer of more than $1,000 from all US citizens to the banks. Thank you for your donation. Not only had the banks messed up, but also they were able to convince us that they were too big to fail.

Let's look at the example of Deutsche Bank. Coming up to the financial crisis, it targeted a return on capital employed of 25%. Good news for shareholders. But for depositors, they offered less than 2% interest. Nowadays after the fallout, the new management only aims for a "moderate" 12%, which seems a lot more reasonable.

We see while banks have enabled the progress mankind has made for millennia, there have been grave excesses harming many people. I am pointing this out because I want you to be very weary when dealing with banks as they don't necessarily share your interests. Their main interest is to generate profit for themselves.

So what can you do? Do you have a free checking account? If not, go get one. Oh, and what do your transaction fees look like? Make sure there are none. Generally, the more you do online, the cheaper you can get. The bank makes enough money on the interest it earns from working with the money you put into your account. Remember, it is effectively a loan you grant your bank.

Then also watch out that you never spend more than you own to avoid overdraft or bounced check fees. They usually range from $20 to $35 in the United States. At current interest levels of about 2% for a money market account, that means you are losing the entire return of an invested $1,000. So if you run the risk of an overdraft, transfer some funds from your savings into your checking account or otherwise restrict your spending.

The same applies for all other fees. They are a key source of income for your bank. While your checking account might be free—as in no monthly fee—ample creative fees might be hidden in the terms. They might be complicated but worth the read, even if it only saves you from paying one single fee. (Read more on finding a good bank account in Ramit Sethi's aforementioned book.)

It is widely known that we tend to put off decisions that are too complex and rather settle for the default. Banks and credit card companies know about this and thus do not expect us to read the terms. When we select a credit card, we get a sheet with terms, which we do not read because we do not understand it. Then we are hit by unexpected fees. We are annoyed by those hidden fees. Really annoyed. But we stick with the card because we believe that other card companies will have equivalent hidden fees. So we are rational in a way. But stupid. There are fair products on the market too. Find them and go through the effort of understanding the terms with all hidden fees and gems. Make sure not to incur the fees and benefit from the gems. My Amex, for instance, comes with a return protection. I never really knew until recently, and I have used it since. Great service — one phone call saved me $40.

Remember the last time you signed up for some online service and checked that you had read and agreed to the terms and conditions. I bet you lied. Maybe it's worth wondering what you agree to, at least in cases that can have serious financial impact on your life.

Commitments: Budgeting, Subscriptions, and Bulk

Reevaluate Good Resolutions
Do you set a certain amount of money aside each month for specific types of expenditures? Say you earmark $50 for movie nights out? While the idea of doing something to manage your expenses was certainly a good one, budgeting also makes it easier for you to spend the $50. Some portion of it will then go to unnecessities such as oversized popcorn and thereby actually diminish the number of your overall moviegoing experiences. If we budget, the money is already spent in our mind; therefore, actually handing it over does not register with us anymore. This is the reason I strongly discourage you from using specific budgets. (This is not a license for unlimited spending!)

Even if you are running a business, budgeting might be something to consider abandoning. A lot of research has been done in the field of "Beyond Budgeting"; and successful companies such as American Express, Google, Toyota, and Whole Foods have said good-bye to traditional budgeting. And so can you.

Subscribing to the Right Service

"Monday 28 April. gym visits 0, no. of gym visits so far this year 1, cost of gym membership per year £370; cost of single gym visit £123." That is what Bridget Jones penned in her eponymous diary. Are you a member of a local YMCA or a gym? Do you own a time-share vacation property? What about your cell phone minutes? *Overconfidence* makes us think we use them more than we actually do, and thus we are initially happy to overpay. The good news is you can change or cancel all these plans right now. And for your time-share, when you sell it, your buyer will be haunted by the same curse of overconfidence!

Let's have a closer look at phone plans. American consumers waste a whopping $13 billion on inflated cell phone plans each year. How big is your piece of that pie? How many minutes do you use a month? You don't know? I understand how painful it is to look at all those complicated phone bills with all their individual items, so you do not look at them. Who can understand a 10–15 page phone bill as AT&T regularly used to send me? You can! Take a deep breath and go get your last few phone bills. If you don't have them anymore, chances are you can download them off your carrier's website.

We are usually biased and select ourselves in a category that is too costly for us. So how many minutes did your research show you needed each month? Now, check what other packages are available and see if you would fit into one of the cheaper ones. You are scared that you might be making more calls next month? That's overconfidence all over again.

Based on lots of research, all these offers have been designed specifically to benefit from the consumers' overconfidence and are driving you into one that is significantly too large. Or did you think it was coincidence that there just wasn't any package that exactly fitted your needs? This goes way beyond phone plans. Think about warranty packages, magazine subscription terms, glossybox type businesses and much more.

If you rightsize all your plans throughout your life, I am sure you can save a ton of money, and that will be well enough to pay for the eventual overage charges for the few times you were actually "underconfident."

Understanding What You Subscribe To

A while back, I looked at two phone plans: A two-year one that cost $90 a month and a second one priced at only $70 a month. The amount $70 or $90 a month does not sound too bad, does it?

What really happens is that the carrier uses the *framing technique*, reframing from a two-year price to a monthly price. It has been shown that we can comprehend the utility of a purchase much better if it's framed this way. One could also say we are fooled more easily as the number is much lower. What we really have to compare are not a $70 and a $90 plan but $1,680 versus $2,160 plus potential other fees and taxes. This is about a $500 difference instead of a $20. That is well worth thinking about carefully. You could visit one of your friends across the country for being a little more considerate with the phone. Especially since most carriers will allow you to migrate to a more expensive plan if you need it later on anyway, there is hardly a good reason to start off high.

Another question to consider is whether you really need a plan with a phone. I found that getting the phone separately was much cheaper and offered more flexibility to get a new model at a later point. More on this in the chapter about "free" stuff.

How about subscription durations? Oftentimes, lower monthly rates are offered for longer commitments. Let me give you an example of what my new ballroom dancing club has to offer:

- 3 month auto-renewing membership €36 per month
- 6 month auto-renewing membership €32 per month

I love dancing and will probably be around for a while, so which one did I pick?

Well, the 6-month option saves €4 a month. That is €48 a year. So of course that's the one to pick. Wait a minute. What if I ever stop dancing there? In the last 15 years, I have never lived anywhere for more than 3 years. Statistically speaking, I will have to cancel in midterm. With the 3-month option, that translates into an overpayment of 1.5 months; and for the 6-month option, that's 3 full months. At the respective rates, that is an overpayment of €54 (= 1.5 × €36) versus €96 (= 3 × €32). So in the end, the cheap option can be expected to be €42 more expensive. That is about a year's worth of savings that gets eaten up upon cancellation. Therefore, I would say it only makes sense for me if I am sure to stay considerably longer than one year. As I know that I will probably want to start dancing with a different partner by then, there is no way I will pick the 6-month option. (Romance spoiler: I don't necessarily change partners all the time, but in this situation where I have just moved to a new city, I just don't expect to keep dancing with the first girl I meet until the end of time. If I still end up doing so and she becomes the love of my life, the few euros for the "wrong" package were well spent.)

Finally — back to overconfidence — with me knowing how busy I am traveling and doing other things and considering that my partner might have to cancel on me occasionally too, it is probably worth considering the seemingly expensive single-session drop-in fee.

Now would actually be a good time to reevaluate existing gym and club memberships. But if you really want to increase your frequency of attending the gym, canceling the membership is not the solution. So I suggest cheating yourself into attending regularly. Check out the last chapter for more on self-control. And get ripped!

Buying Bulk

Purchase all items and services that you can store in bulk. Buying an annual supply of noodles, rice, toilet paper, toothpaste, and so on can be worth it. After shopping once, you can go worry-free for the rest of the year and without further time- and gas-costly rides to the store or shipping charges. And if you try, you can even get a bulk discount. You will know you have overdone it when you start leasing additional storage space though.

Here is a quick example that this also applies to things you cannot store physically. I love going to the sauna, and I know I end up going there at least twice a month. Each visit rings up at €16. The facility, however, offers a prepaid deal where you can buy a pass for €240 that will subsequently give you a 20% discount on each visit. That means each visit will only cost me €12.80. I know that only very few regulars purchase the pass as they think €240 is way too much money for a sauna ticket. Let's look at the math:

- Investment: €240
- Value: (€240 / €12.80 =) 18.75 visits, which translates to a value of €300 at the regular price (18.75 × €16)
- Annual visits: 24 – Thus one pass is good for a little over 9 months (18.75 / 24 × 12).
- Return on invest per year: (300 / 240 – 1) / 3 × 4 = 33%

Yes, that prepaid pass, which costs "so" much money, offers me a pretty much risk-free return of 33% over the course of a year. There is no bank in the world to beat that. Even if I had to take out some credit card debt, it would still be a value-creating deal. By knowing this, and knowing your future desires, you can save a lot of money by spending early.

A word of caution: Spend your money on something else if you do not have a steady track record of going to the sauna. The pass will not help to discipline you into going there, although you might hope just that. See overconfidence right above.

Paying

Money is a curious thing. We said it was but an idea, a strange one though. Let me recount a story that Dan Ariely presented during one of his talks in

Berkeley in 2011. At an MIT dorm, he put a soda into a fridge and waited. Every day he checked until someone had taken his soda. In another experiment, he put a dollar bill into the same fridge and waited again. What do think happened? It hardly took a day in a busy college dorm for the soda to disappear. However, the dollar bill had an amazing tendency to remain in place.

Apparently, physical cash can raise to our awareness things we would otherwise simply let slip. Dan was so fascinated that he set out to write an entire book merely on this. Check out *The (Honest) Truth About Dishonesty*. There he concludes that the more detached some action is from physical money, the more likely we are to rationalize it even if it is immoral.

How do you feel about taking a pencil at the office? How do you feel about taking $0.10 out of petty cash at the office to buy one? Now look at all the fancy instruments created by the financial industry and give the financial crisis a second thought.

We are very honest to ourselves whenever it involves actual cash. Let us call this the *cash care effect*. So you will want to create an environment where you deal with as much physical cash as possible — even as this gets more and more difficult in an ever-more-computerized world.

The physical act of handing over cash and not getting it back is psychologically more painful than handing over a debit or credit card, which you will get back. This goes back to our loss aversion. Therefore, various payment methods vary in their ease or respectively their difficulty of payment. We call this effect *friction*. Also, they vary by how much the consumption is coupled with an act of payment and thus facilitate or inhibit purchases. Combined with the mental accounting described before, this can get quite perverse: A lady sees an expensive cashmere sweater in a store and decides not to buy it as it would be beyond her means. When she gets it for her birthday from her husband, she is more than happy, even though they keep only a joint bank account. Here she can enjoy it because the act of paying is decoupled from the act of consumption, and the money spent on the sweater is not in her mental account.

Companies such as credit card issuers or Square and Google Wallet all aim at benefiting from these effects. PayPal nowadays asks only for your e-mail address and swooshes the money out of you credit cards. A perfect thing if you are in bed and your wallet is downstairs, as Matt shared in one of my online posts. How much easier can it get? And so PayPal's Express Checkout has been shown to increase sales by 18% as compared to the time before it was offered as a means of payment. Even more evolved is Apple's app store. It has your credit card data, and you can disable all warnings so you can just click and enjoy. And then it's "Oops, I purchased something" once you see your credit card bill — if you even look at it.

A debit card will hurt you sooner as it hits your bank account right away. But nothing works for you as well as going to the ATM. It reminds you that you have spent a certain amount of money. It is the modern way of repenting for your sins.

Try to be aware of these leaks in your wallet and their size. By paying as much as you can through a single channel, whether that is cash (for extremists) or just one debit or credit card. If self-control is tough for you, go for the cash-only option. It will weaken your spending pleasure to a degree that it might even prevent consumption altogether in some cases. The miles or points you collect might cost you way more than you think. If you choose the card, make sure you read each statement carefully and think about each purchase once again as your read it. This way, you can train yourself.

I know a girl who has a red sticker on her credit card, which screams "stop" in her mind. This might help you too feel some more payment pain as you hand it over and thus improve your decision-making process. Even leaving your plastic at home, unless you are heading for a specific purchase, could offer some remedy. Along the same logic, deactivate all sorts of one-click purchases at Amazon.com, Apple, etc.

Furthermore, it is not bad character if you decide not to make a purchase at the register. But you might want to be nice and at least ask the cashier if it's OK to leave the item there or if you should put it back.

You might start thinking that I hate credit cards. Of course we need a credit card, and I have several myself. At least if you live in the United States and many other countries, there is no way around having one if you want to rent a car or book a hotel, for instance. Other than that, credit cards come with many benefits—miles and points or the ability to track spending online with mint.com or similar services. That's why many financial self-help books recommend them so strongly. Yet the disadvantages, i.e., behavioral risks, are widely underappreciated. By the way, there are many other macroeconomic arguments against them that go beyond the scope of this title. To learn more, read the book *Freefall* by Joseph E. Stiglitz.

Saving for a New Versailles

What I have described in this section is a potential explanation for the nation's savings rates. In the United States, where a lot of people still get a paper paycheck, you have a feeling of luck each pay period. "Here is the hard-earned money." But there is no feeling of the money being spent as it mostly goes out by credit card. In Europe where everyone is paid by wire transfer without any notice, there is no feeling of money coming in, thus no "Now I can spend it" mind-set. Instead, there is a tough feeling of forking over cash all the time.

Consequently, from 2000 to 2008, Europeans saved between 5.5% and 7.4% of their money, and Americans between 1.5% and 3.8%. France is the savings champion with rates between 11.4% and 13.7%. Imagine what saving an additional 4% (difference between American and European) of your income during your entire life span would mean. Then think about another 6% as the answer why the French have Versailles.

Prepaid Irrationalities

Prepaying is related to the above forms of commitment. The main difference is that your commitment is so strong that instead of just earmarking an amount or signing for it, you actually pay in advance. This little difference, however, makes prepayment by an order of magnitude stronger than simple budgeting.

A prepaid consumption — e.g., Internet, phone service, all-you-can-eat dinner — makes you experience the paying completely separately from the act of consumption. Friction is at a minimum. You can almost consume as if it was free. We derive a lot of pleasure from these totally decoupled sales, to the extent that we often overconsume. Ever had a little too much at the all-you-can-eat Chinese restaurant around the corner? We love not having to worry about paying while we consume. We enjoy this so much that we actually prefer to pay up front — even if what we pay is more than what we would have paid if charged by the real consumption afterward.

Let me give a detailed example: John, after his 25-year college reunion, goes out and buys a red two-seater convertible, financed with a standard car loan. Although the car performs well, he realizes that the occasions for driving it are rarer than anticipated and the pleasure of recreating the college feeling fades quickly. Soon the monthly payments are nothing more than a painful reminder of a costly indulgence. The monthly bill seems to be exaggerated as compared to the occasional driving weekend. After a few painful months, he decides to go to the bank and pay off the loan completely. Well, now that he owns the car, he is no longer worried about driving a certain amount each month — driving feels free to him. He enjoys it again and even revels in looking at the pristine vehicle in his driveway.

Analyzing the situation, there are a few striking points. First of all, if he had had the money for the full purchase all along, he should have bought the car outright as the interest and loan fees most likely were unnecessary expenses. For a moment, let's consider that those costs were negligible or simply ignored by John. Then however, it should not make a difference whether the car is owned, leased, or financed in regard to the pleasure he derives. But it did. The pain of paying and the pain of debt hurt him so much that he disliked the car and instead chose to give up a lot of liquidity—a value in itself—without getting any tangible additional value.

For the same reason, the lease offers sound better initially (low payment now) as compared to the purchase in full (huge payment now). The full effect of the ongoing payments is discounted too much, i.e., in a *hyperbolic* way to use some jargon. Unfortunately, when you want something, you have to bite the bullet eventually. Do it now; it only makes you stronger.

There are a few more situations where you might unknowingly be subject to the effects of prepayment. In casinos and on vacations to faraway countries with different currencies, we typically change our dollars for some tokens or local currency. Can you guess what that means? The pain of paying is experienced at the point of exchange; afterward we spend rather worry-free. In the end, oftentimes we find ourselves spending all our tokens or currency long before it is time to return home.

In some instances we face a partial prepayment. Deutsche Bahn, the German railroad, offers a product called BahnCard 50, which allows the customer after spending €240 to get half off all standard fares during the course of one year. So this product decouples part of the ticket spending from the consumption and makes riding a train seem like a great deal. How much it really saves is hard to tell as it does not apply to the multitude of special deals the company offers. So if you see something like this, think at least twice before buying it. In the past, I only bought it, when I was almost paying it off with the first trip I made and was convinced that more trips would follow. In case of doubt, I do not buy it. Although every time I travel, I have to live with the feeling of being excluded from the club, as the ticket vendor, the conductor, and just about everybody else ask me whether I have a BahnCard.

Gambling

How much is the current Mega Millions jackpot? What is more relevant than the potential win are the odds of it really materializing. That is why that jackpot billboard sign on your way home at night is so intriguing. Winning $100 million? Would not that be uberamazing? It would, but truth be told, it will not happen. The chances of winning in these kinds of lotteries are lower than one in billions or even straight zero (zero, really) as found in Virginia a few years ago. A funny comparison that Daniel Crosby made during his TEDxHuntsville talk is that you are 24 times more likely to be executed by your state than win Mega Millions. You are also 3 times more likely to be put on death row and then be pardoned by your governor. Can't relate to that? It is still more likely that you will be crushed to death by a TV set than win Mega Millions.

The result is actually quite sad: Lotteries are changing the relative distribution of money from the poorer part of the population to the richer one. In this way, they work in the opposite of most government redistribution programs such as progressive taxes. This happens because a larger proportion of the low-income population plays the lottery in the *hope* of striking it big. Not only do they play more—they also spend up to four times as much per ticket.[4] For obvious reasons, the higher-income brackets are less enticed by that prospect.

But lotteries are not a good way to get rich by playing. They are a great business for those offering gambles as to the hope comes overconfidence — the sister of risk aversion. It has been found that we are on average willing to spend more for a lottery than the average win. We cherish winning so much and are so sure about it that we overpay for the opportunity to win. If someone offered you a bet where you would win $77 in 1 out of 8 times, how much would you be willing to pay? Mathematically, your average win would be $77 / 8, which is $9.63. Of course this is not easily computable in your head. So most people offer considerably more. The casino pockets the difference.

Lifestyle Fasting Today and Tomorrow

Jason, a fellow student of mine at one of America's top business schools, had thrown out all his dirty dishes and silverware that were piling up in the kitchen sink when he left his former New England home. Instead, he chose to use only disposable ones from then on. The prospect of never having to wash up enthused him. But imagine the cost. What he saved in time, he clearly lost in money. The waste certainly did not help the environment either.

---

[4] While only 28% of Americans earn less than $40k/year a full 54% of lottery players make less than $40k/year.

How would you describe your lifestyle? What does it mean financially? What impact does it have on your time?

For now, list what you really need to survive. And here I mean "survive" as in "not die." If you do this honestly, you will see that it is not much compared to all you inventoried before. This new list is your *minimum lifestyle*. Everything else is a bonus you deserve being excited about. You can find more on minimalist living in Leo Babauta's writings at zenhabits.com, but here is my take on things.

If you have ever fasted, you will know how sweet it is to resume eating what you have refused for a certain period. This approach you can use for your entire life. Temporarily cut all spending that is nonessential for two months every year. Live as close to your minimum lifestyle as possible. You will feel amazing afterward.

In the process, do not create a pent-up demand for assets or things that you really need. If your dishwasher is broken, have it repaired. But do not go out and buy a blender just because you think making smoothies would be nice. Also, do not buy any newspapers or movie tickets. No dining out, etc. You think you will be unhappy during those two months? Poor people can be happy. My grandma still tells us how glad they all were at Christmas when all they had were a few cookies. Fasting establishes a baseline that allows for more profound happiness and enjoyment once you resume consumption. On top of that, it saves a lot of money and time. While fasting, you will learn that going out with friends can be fun even without drinking. You will be rewarded with new self-discipline, which can help you in all areas of life. After two months, you will be used to it and everything you do after that will feel new and like a gift.

Personally, I have eventually settled on living way below my theoretical means. I can tell from experience it feels much better to live in an apartment that is not cluttered. The things I have are of true value to me — my prized possessions: That one watch I inherited from my grandfather is no longer one among many. That piece of artwork someone special gifted me from abroad is not be tarnished by a surrounding glutton of glassware. Plus it is so much easier to clean. I break fewer items. And that is a reduced source of unhappiness.

Admittedly, on the other hand, I have hundreds of books and more clothes than any man I know. Those I want, I cherish and enjoy. Yet if a piece of garment is broken beyond repair or a book is really not of any value (and I decide that regularly), it is preferably donated or goes to trash.

Source: Courtesy of Jonathan Fields

In the last 15 years, I have lived in seven countries for time frames of several months to several years each. This has been a huge force in understanding the true value of things and more so of people and relationships. On my first trips, I still brought little trinkets home. On the last few trips, I returned with humble memories and plenty of photographs. If you do not need it, do not buy it. Don Aslett, in his book *Clutter's Last Stand*, discusses at length that value comes from using not from owning things. "No matter how you look at it, clutter is a poor investment." Otherwise, you might end up with that giant huge red dumpster in front of your home. "This is what is left of someone's life. Not the experiences, but the stuff," as Jonathan Fields moans. But experiences are more likely to make you happy than material goods. Plus they do not take up further space and maintenance time. You get all the value without any residual clutter. Also, seeking memories that you get from experiences makes you an interesting person to be around. That, finally, is a true symbol of status and an image you cannot buy.

Once you have established lifestyle fasting as an anchor point in your life, you will see that this can be your ticket to escaping the bigger-better-more rat race and changing to a "happiness cycle." You will feel better overall with less and save more in the long run. Ultimately, you will overtake all your friends caught up in the rat race. This extra turbo to building a fortune makes perfect sense.

Lifetime cash need

Here is a little back-of-the-envelope calculation on your lifetime cash needs, starting with your retirement prospects. It will show you how much money you will need eventually. Since this topic could easily fill a library of its own, let me just tell you that for myself, a thirty-something male, I have found that there is little to expect from social welfare once I retire. So it is better to save far more than the $50-$150 a month that some financial institutions are trying to sell retirement plans for.

Behavioral economics research has shown that we tend to significantly underestimate the amounts we will be needing, and our financial consultants are not doing any better. This is due to the above-mentioned effect of *hyperbolic discounting*. Subconsciously, we do not correctly value future needs versus present needs. Consequentially, while we typically save to retire early, we are hardly able to do so because we just have not saved enough. Take your current monthly spending, add 3% per year until your desired retirement age to account for inflation, and add another say 50% on top. This will account for additional medical bills, travel, and you having much more time to spend money. So what does that number look like? That is about as much as you will want to have in your bank account upon retirement to take out — every month!

If at this point you are not completely devastated yet, add the cost of your dream wedding, raising kids, building a house and the other major life events to your list.

Key Points to Remember

- Go through the process described in this chapter once a year or at least every time there is a substantial change in your life, such as a move or change of whom you live with, etc. I find time during my fasting period.

- By now, you are well aware of your *financial income* and *spending* as well as the relationship between *money* and *time* in your life as illustrated in a simple form by the *one-hour rule*. If you have not written this down yet, do it now.

- *Loss aversion*: Our fear of losing what we have makes us spend a lot of time protecting it. Consequently, we do not have enough time to earn more. As most of the things you try to protect against are random anyway, the protection is mostly an illusion (see also illusion of control in the chapter before). Stop protecting; start earning. There are more riches in the world for you to win than you own to lose today.

- *Risk aversion*: Our subconscious hates risks, and we pay for insurances to rid us of them. For the insurance company to be profitable, it absolutely has to charge more than the materialization of these risks will eventually cost. Therefore, take out only policies that insure absolutely life-threatening risks.

- *Selective perception* opens our mental filters and makes us notice certain things over proportionally often. If you suddenly see something happen around you all the time, check whether it really occurs more frequently. It might just be an illusion.

- Banks too are in it to make money. So find a bank with free checking account and do not put blind faith in their investment advisers. Read the terms for everything you sign and make up your mind.
- *Budgeting* can help save money, but it can also lead to overspending. Therefore, refrain from overly specific budgets.
- *Overconfidence*: We vastly overestimate the frequency of desired activities and usage of certain items. (Think gym attendance or magazine reading). Change your subscriptions and memberships to a minimum.
- *Framing* is used to make goods and services look cheaper by presenting them in a different way, e.g., monthly price instead of full purchase price. Look at your total cost and also check the implications of the duration and cancellation policies. Then before making a purchase reframe the decision with your *one-hour-rule* and compare it to what else you could be getting for the same investment.
- Buy bulk wherever the savings are worth it, considering space and cash availability.
- *Cash care effect*: Whenever cash is involved, the issue has a bigger chance of being raised to our consciousness. Create an environment where you deal with as much cash as possible. Handing over cash is the most difficult way of spending money; it therefore creates a lot of so-called *friction*. You will want this friction as close as possible to the event of consumption to minimize spending, thus avoid prepayment or bill-me-later.
- *Hope* makes us fight for a better future and put faith in lotteries, which are effectively an income

distribution from the poor to the rich. So never ever gamble.

- You should now know what your *minimum lifestyle* looks like, what you truly need to simply survive. Schedule a month or two right now when you are going to live it. Afterward, live below your theoretical means.

- *Hyperbolic discounting*: We tend to significantly underestimate the amounts we will be needing down the road, and our financial consultants are not doing any better. Do some realistic math instead of gut estimates.

CAUGHT IN A WEB OF

URGES

In this part ...

You learn about true and imagined needs as well the emotional attraction that spurs desire. The Nobel Prize–winning prospect theory invites you to look at expectations in a new light. And we will see how values, colors, shapes, and sexual tension short-circuit our brains to make us seek what we actually don't want. And of course we add a few more silver bullets to our toolkit to make you invulnerable to harmful ideas. All that is broken down into intelligible bits.

Ambition

"'Would you tell me, please,
which way I ought to go from here?'
'That depends a good deal on where you want to get to,'
said the Cat.
'I do not much care where—' said Alice.
'Then it does not matter which way you go,' said the Cat."
—Lewis Carroll, *Alice in Wonderland*
"I imagined everything. I never thought it would happen."
Keith Richards, *Life*

Finding Our True Needs

After creating a clean base to start from in the last chapter, it is best to know where you want to go in the long run to be able to determine the best way to get there. Retirement is only one thing to save for. There is much more. Your next car; an apartment, condo, or house you would like to own; a new stereo; or iMac. Start saving money for those expenses in advance and they will be much cheaper.

In the introduction, I had asked you to create a list of what you aspire your perfect life to look like. Look at your list—I bet it is long. There are many things we want, we deem to need. At least that was my experience when I saw people put together such lists. Have you ever wondered why? We will get there later.

First, let us revisit our minimum lifestyle from the last chapter, which I assume should be much shorter than the list from the introduction. Yet I bet your minimum lifestyle list is still way too long. Therefore, we are going to look at a few ways of determining whether you really need something.

What kind of honest needs are there? In the early '40s of the last century, Abraham Maslow created his theory of human motivation, which is often depicted as the pyramid shown below. He postulated that all needs can be put into one of five categories—i.e., physiological, safety, love/belonging, esteem, and self-actualization. Multiple motivations can coexist at any time, and one might or might not be dominant. Maslow showed that we should seek fulfillment starting at the bottom of the pyramid. This means, for instance, that we should take care of being well-nourished first before we take on safety. Once we are safe (and fed), we should focus on relationships and so on. By following our desires in this way, we can get more value for our money.

The need for self-actualization is particularly interesting. "What a man can be, he must be" is how he put it. For him, this is accomplishing everything that one can. Getting the max out of yourself, whether it is becoming CEO of your company, the best parent in the world, or the fastest race car driver. It is the desire that has made you buy this book. A desire that you can only fulfill indirectly by attaining all other goals.

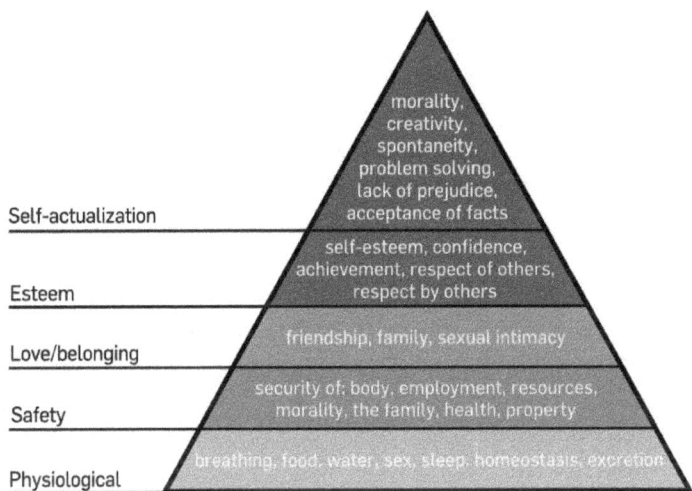

Source: Wikipedia, Licence CC BY-SA 3.0

How to Choose the Right Thing

As we have seen, rationally speaking, we want things as a means to an end. What end are you trying to achieve? This question is your key to make sane purchasing decisions. Instead of spending money, once you have determined the desire that you seek to fulfill with the purchase at hand, you can also consider options other than purchasing that very item in that particular place.

1. Positive procrastination
I once fell for a $79 upgrade offer to a software package when I reinstalled my computer. I figured, I wanted everything to be up-to-date. What a mistake.

Had I paused to think twice, I would have realized that I never used this software for months prior to that day — and even worse, I have not used it since. Since then, whenever I see something that awakens an urge in my mind to go out and buy it, the following rule has proven to be very beneficial: wait at least a day.

Why not use one of our fallacies to our benefit? We always tend to postpone things that should be done. So why not put off some of the things we shouldn't be doing? After the first day then, you might say you have already been waiting a day. Maybe you can wait a little more. If you don't need to buy it now, wait. Maybe the demand perishes in the process.

While you procrastinate, ponder on the true cost with the following questions, knowing that we have a tendency only to look at pro arguments to supply us with an OK for our desire:

- What additional cost is involved using the item? Think razor blades, printer cartridges, fuel, taxes, etc.
- How to discard the item? What cost or profit does that add?
- How much does it cost in respect to my annual income and to my total net worth? Apply the one-hour rule. Buying something takes just a second, even if you have worked for hours to be able to afford it.
- How often will I be using it? We often overestimate out of overconfidence. Therefore, put it one category lower than you had spontaneously intended.
- How much time will I spend using it? What else am I missing out on instead?

- In what possibly creative ways could I use it? For instance, a sofa is not only a place to sit but also a piece of furniture to look at that creates some atmosphere in your home.
- How long can I keep it? Watch out as this heavily depends on the quality of the product you choose.
- What is the cost per use? Finally, you might need to take out your pocket calculator. Looking at my furniture, I can see a bed and a sofa. Both cost about $4,000 back in 2006. A hefty amount. But they are the most comfy waterbed and beautiful designer sofa. Both I have had for seven years, which translates to about $570 annually. However, per use the picture is totally different. While I have possibly spent 1,800 nights in my bed, the cost per use so far was $2. However, I am not sure if I have sat 100 times on that sofa. That's a rocking $40 for every time my butt touched the leather! The only good news is that both are still in shape to last at least another seven years, which will help me work on getting the cost per use down.

Still want it? Read on.

Note: I asked you to procrastinate, but while you are spending conscious time on the decision, my advice is to hurry up. Decision time is a cost as well, and you could have fun with your friends or make some money during that time instead. The amount of time you spend here should be proportional to the amount you are planning to spend.

2. Asset-light approach
Based on the cost-per-use idea, paying per use would be ideal. However, that concept is a little tricky

to apply to sofas. But look at tools, for example. Instead of buying a power drill, you might just rent one every time you need it. This can turn a $300 decision into a $20 one about which you do not need to worry too much. You do not buy a truck just because you move once every few years. U-Haul does the job—nationwide. This is even more relevant for goods that depreciate quickly, like buying a DSLR for your vacation. Bad news, next year everyone will have a nicer one. So better rent it this year and who knows maybe next year you do not want to take pictures anyway.

Just think about the stuff you have sold in the chapter above after some initial use and how much value you lost in the process.

Can it get better still? Instead of driving to the store, getting your above-mentioned power drill, driving back home, and the going back to return it, why not borrow it from your neighbor? Suddenly, meeting a stranger does not seem such a worthless prospect. You might even meet an exciting person.

Now your $300 decision turned out a free power drill—although a six-pack of beer might be a good relationship investment upon returning the tool.

3. Consider alternatives
If the above didn't yield satisfyingly cheap results, why not think out of the box? It is the solution that you truly seek, not the thing. For instance, you can hang pictures with stick-on hooks instead of drilling a hole into your drywall. Instead of hotels, there are Airbnb.com or even CouchSurfing.com. There are many alternatives once you start looking beyond mainstream options.

How about getting rid of your dryer or not buying one once the current one breaks down? It will save the purchase cost, reduce wear on your garments, and thus you will be able keep them more than twice as long. It saves electricity. And time. Wait, you thought a dryer saves time? Not necessarily. After taking things out of the dryer, you still need to fold them before putting them into the closet. So instead of putting them into the dryer, hang them on a rack along the future main folding line, and then as you pick them up, keep them folded the way they are on the rack, fold them again at the secondary folding lines, and put them away. This actually takes less time than putting them from the washer to the dryer and then folding them. Makes sense? It does, although dryer manufacturers spend a lot of money making us believe otherwise. Well, if you want to keep your dryer because you like the fluffiness of towels coming out of it, fine. Just do not use it for anything else and have the best of both worlds.

4. Right size

Is bigger really better? Our *size bias* certainly makes us believe it is. We rather choose a larger option than the smaller thing because it makes us feel bigger and more powerful. Can you imagine Arnold Schwarzenegger step out of a Fiat? No, he drives — or at least drove — a Hummer, which is basically a tank. And so we buy expensive gas-guzzling SUVs as they feel safe, despite them actually having a worse passenger injury record than regular cars.

Ask yourself, would the object of your desire yield more than what you aimed for originally? Will a blender with 2000 W really be so much better than one with 1000 W? Or will it just consume more power and allow chopping hardwood, which you never do anyway? How often and what do you use it for? This is what it should be sized to do. Everything else will come at a cost without return, even if the power increment comes at only a few dollars. As Benjamin Franklin noted, "A penny saved is a penny earned." So beware of your overconfidence as you define the requirements.

One summer day in the '80s, construction workers pulled up to a lot near our house. They had brought the big rig. Hardly had I ever seen such a humongous construction project in our middle-class residential area. But the palacelike building was completed in time for winter. When we visited the new neighbors, we noticed that the interior was far from completed, and they barely had any furniture. Curious it got when this had not changed a year later. The family was kind and always invited the neighbors over to their little pool outside. The man of the house was an entrepreneur always talking about his amazing business. He was so adamant about being the top earner on the block that he owned a prestigious vehicle and moved it to the roadside whenever he knew we had visitors. However, the car did not even have an engine anymore as he could not afford to have it fixed. His desire to prove his wealth in a neighborhood that was just a little bit too upscale finally drove him into personal bankruptcy. He died a broken man, leaving a sad family behind. I am convinced, had he moved to a poorer area instead, they all might be happy today.

Where did you settle down? Living in a neighborhood where people are on average wealthier than yourself might sound tempting. It is probably very safe, well-kept, and inspiring. Yet it will be not only too expensive but also too frustrating in the long run. If you move to a richer neighborhood after your promotion, this will make your "step up the ladder" actually feel bad. It is better to earn more first, and when you outearn your neighborhood significantly, think about moving to another one that is slightly below your income level. That way, you have the benefit of feeling "I made it," and you can still enjoy feeling rich by outspending your neighbors.

5. Configure

Once the base item is rightsized, oftentimes there are options to pick. Does your new Dell laptop really need the integrated card reader option? Options are a treacherous trick. We all love them, the warranty option protects us, the additional ports on our new laptop ensure compatibility to devices we might later decide to buy. But they are all costly. We pay for the physical option as well as the opportunity cost of not being able to buy something else. Plus you wasted your time deciding upon which options to pick. Studies have shown that most likely you will never even use the options, which means you have greatly overvalued them during the decision-making process. Therefore, start with the no-frills model of whatever you need, never buy the warranty, and only pick those options that you need right now or are 100% required in the near future. Be honest to yourself and your wallet. To say it more drastically, rather spend the money for a faster CPU than for the warranty. If the computer really breaks, it will not kill you, but a slow CPU will kill you certainly — gradually that is — over the next few years stealing you ever so small bits of time.

Regarding options to an already-expensive base item, it has been shown that our demand elasticity decreases. That means we are more willing to pay for an option to a base item than we would for the same feature stand-alone, i.e., without the base item. In our mind, we think that since we are already spending a large chunk of money, the little option will not make a difference anymore. That is why some homeowner policies offer paint-spill protection options for DIYers and credit card fraud protection options for the first $50 (as everything else is covered by the credit card company anyway). Many more little useless options can be found in the marketplace. This is what is called *integration of losses* by Richard Thaler.

Because of this, we often take out duplicate insurances. So many credit cards and other programs come with an accident insurance or travel insurance at very little surcharge. Sounds good, so we take it and forget. When we are offered a new one or when we actually could file a claim, we cannot remember. We end up signing up for many of them that all go unused.

6. Reuse

You know what you want. So why not buy used, pre-owned, or refurbished items?

You might be afraid that the product is damaged, has not been taken care of very well, and will thus break soon. It might be dirty and full of germs. Components might have been replaced with inferior-quality ones. There are thousands of potential risks in buying pre-owned. However, if you buy a lot of used items, you diversify that risk. Maybe one in a hundred used DVDs does not play anymore. Annoying, isn't it? But if you had bought all of them brand-new, you would have spent several hundred dollars more!

If you are considering expensive merchandise, it will be important for you to be able to investigate and assess the quality of the item prior to purchasing. An Apple MacBook could be such an item, where you don't feel like just running the risk of buying a used one, unless you are a computer engineer. What you could still do is have a look at http://store.apple.com/us/browse/home/specialdeals/mac. Apple sells certified pre-owned products with warranty at a hefty discount.

Even more can be saved with cars. On average, a car loses 9% of its value just by driving off the lot. An additional 10% is lost during the first year. A pre-owned can thus be an amazing deal. The dealership certification might just make this emotionally acceptable if you don't have a friend who is a mechanic.

Of course these warranties come at a price. So you will have to check if a pre-owned with warranty is still worth it compared to a new one with factory warranty.

Using Your Mind to Choose

How much time are you willing or able to spend finding alternatives? Consider you are looking for a rental property. You find two properties that are virtually identical except the following. In scenario A, there are two options with one being a slightly inferior form of the other:

x: $290 and 25 minutes to work
x': $330 and 25 minutes to work

In scenario B, the two alternatives vary largely:

x: $290 and 25 minutes to work

y: $350 and 7 minutes to work

Assuming that you have neither extremely strong preferences for saving some money or commute, how would you behave in each scenario? Are you going to pick one of them or continue looking for an apartment, knowing that someone else might lease either or both of the two current options in the meantime?

In a study, 64% of the participants looked for additional options in scenario B, but only 40% continued their search in scenario A. While we cannot say whether x or y are better in scenario B, we can say for sure that x is better than x'.

The general finding was that we rather procrastinate or search for other options when the decision is difficult. Whenever it's easy, we pick one. However, in both cases there might be other options available that are better to what you have seen so far.

Next time you look for an apartment, get an overview of the market first, see what is available in general, and build some sort of expectation of what you will find by continuing to look. A decision that seems simple might appear as such because you are only looking at a limited part of the environment. The best alternatives are often hidden in difficult decisions, and you might not feel as comfortable with them right away. Losing an alternative might feel bad due to the ownership bias but is probably not an issue because many new properties go on the market continuously, but in other cases it might well be. Finally, make sure you consider the opportunity cost of continuing the search versus the expected value of additional alternatives.

Generally, when there are many options, we tend to stick with the default. When the default is doing nothing, this is good for your wallet, but your desire will go unfulfilled and you will eventually be frustrated. If in turn, the default is the first thing you saw; it is likely not the best choice. So how to decide?

Making the Right Decisions by Choosing the Right Alternatives

When choosing, you can either look at alternatives in a positive way (i.e., which one to pick) or in a negative way (i.e., which one to give up). Image you are planning a vacation and you have found the two options below. You cannot find any more details on them, and in scenario 1, you need to pick one now; otherwise you will not be able to book before your desired departure date. You choose what you prefer.

In scenario 2, you have made a reservation for both packages, and you have to cancel one by today; otherwise you will be billed for both. You choose what to cancel.

How would you decide in both cases? The same questions were asked to two separate groups during a study, and they answered as you can see below.

		Prefer	Cancel
Spot A	• average weather • average beaches • medium-quality hotel • medium-temperature water • average nightlife	33 %	52 %
Spot B	• lots of sunshine • gorgeous beaches and coral reefs • ultra-modern hotel • very cold water • very strong winds • no nightlife	67 %	48 %

Source: Shafir, E., et al. (1993), p. 16

It turned out that a strong majority in scenario 1 preferred vacation B over A. At the same time, canceling either of them was almost equally likely in scenario 2. For the owner of the hotel A, this means they really want you to make a cancelable reservation right away ("no commitment!") because they know that their chances of getting a booking are considerably higher than if they would let you explore other options first.

The rule is that in positive choices (which one to pick), we look for positive qualities, like lots of sunshine, and disregard negative or potentially negative qualities. In turn, for negative choices (which one to give up or which one not to pick, which one to disqualify) we focus on the negative qualities and ignore everything else to a large extent.

Think twice when evaluating two options to make sure you do not feel buyers' remorse later on. Whether a trip, a car, a home, or just about anything else, by making your decision from both perspectives, you can overcome this effect. While it is in part related to the ownership bias, it has also been witnessed when you are choosing a gift for someone else.

Actually Getting It

Once you have determined what you really want to purchase, it is time to decide a couple of things: when and where to buy.

Time

So when is the best time to buy? One of my professors once lectured, "You have to step through the window of opportunity as it opens, not as it closes" — a modern interpretation of the Roman "Carpe diem" (Seize the day). However, for most commercially available items, there is no true window of opportunity anymore. Scarcity is usually an illusion deliberately created by sellers. Most items can be bought today as well as tomorrow or the day after. In the Western Hemisphere, we are blessed to live in a world of abundance. Almost everything can be shipped within a day or two without express charges. Amazon now ships some items within 12 hours. Many software products can be downloaded instantaneously. This abundance was not shared by all people in history, and not even all places and populations today are sharing it. Therefore, this thinking still influences us today. So before giving in to the pressure of a salesperson, consider the true availability of the product. The more you think about it, the more you will realize that you hardly need anything *right now*.

Nonetheless, seasonality matters for some products. Especially food items are big in this category. Raspberries in winter might not be such a good deal. By adapting your eating habits a little bit, you can save a lot and still eat the same amount of everything throughout the year. Additionally, pausing eating certain foods for some months makes you enjoy them more once you resume.

How about deflation and other general price trends? In Japan, we hear a lot about deflation, money becoming worth more over time just by waiting. That is the opposite of the inflation that is going on in most Western countries. But we too see deflation in certain sectors. Moore's law makes computers cheaper every year. Most technology products follow suit. You can wait, or just buy last year's model right away if it fits your demands.

When and where can you expect overstock situations? I saved thousands of dollars in hotel bills with hotwire.com for the company I worked for. They offer last-minute empty-hotel rooms pretty much all over the world. Oh, and despite their terms and conditions, they do issue refunds to valued customers. Just ask.

Location

Now let us look at the where in more detail. There are many discount sites online, so you will want to check those out. But good old brick-and-mortar is still there too. Call up a few stores around you and ask for pricing. Negotiate on the phone—with the manager.

Have them e-mail or fax you a quote if they do not want to give you a price over the phone.

Once you have your best prices, go to the top 2 places, starting with the runner-up, and negotiate again. If you get a better deal at your first stop, take it; otherwise purchase at the originally cheapest outlet.

How global is your footprint? What languages do you speak? If you can, shop in a different country — either in person or online. Globalization has harmonized prices much, but not entirely. Autodesk used to sell its software at a myriad of prices around the world but has now standardized into a few pricing zones.

Virtually equivalent BMWs used to sell for the same figure amount in the United States and in Germany, except in the United States it was dollars, and in Germany euros had to be paid. With one euro buying in excess of $1.40 at the time of this writing, you could get a pretty good deal. This holds true even after shipping and making some minor modifications to get the car on a European standard. Imagine getting a €40K car for €29K + 3K. This is a total savings of 8K or 20%. I am talking after dealer discount. So the original list price would probably have been closer to €46K. (Note that this only works if you actually live in both countries before and after moving the vehicle. Otherwise, you have to pay duties and taxes that largely offset the gain. So this probably only works for "4-hour workweekers" and expats.)

In general, I have found that books, hair care, contact lens products, and IT goods are cheaper in the United States. On the other hand, good food is more affordable in Europe.

As we will see later, prices are mostly arbitrary. There is no justifiable reason for a good deal of the variations in product pricing. Companies sell for the price that allows them to capture the targeted market.

Not all desires start with you in your armchair. You might just be attracted to something in a store you are at. RedLaser is a handy iPhone app. It scans the bar code and shows you the prices of the item all over the world. RedLaser anything you buy that costs more than $10. It might be delivered to your door before you get home—possibly cheaper than in the store you saw it.

Also write shopping lists before you go out to the store. Then stick to them to prevent wants from emerging. Our subconscious is like a little kid. If it is trained that it does not get whatever it wants just by yelling, it will stop yelling.

Great Stuff

"Happiness is an inside job" — William Arthur Ward
20th-century American pastor and author

Above we have discussed what we want. This chapter is about getting us there with the best experience. Let us enjoy what we buy and do to the max.

In these modern times we believe that only what we see is true. And what is true, we see. If it only were that easy. In this chapter, I will show three striking ways we distort our perception.

1. We tend to only see the difference between expectation and fact. (And only if it is stark enough.)
2. We usually get what we expect, as we often refuse to realize and accept any difference between expected and real outcome.
3. We can even change the way we experience fact to further meet our expectation.

1. The Difference Between Expectation and Fact

Take a red piece of paper; hold it in front of a well-lit white wall for a minute. Then suddenly remove it. Remaining will be a green spot where you were holding the paper. The wall is not dirty; your mind is just giving you the difference to its expected red. And in the world of colors, red and green make white.

So what you experience and what you thus judge is merely the difference between your expectation and the fact. I recently found myself in this little pseudoexperiment: In a nondescript dark setting, I was served a dark plastic cup. Expecting it to contain apple juice, it took me a minute to grasp that this was the not rotten apple juice I sensed but real beer! Try it yourself and serve someone expecting coffee a cup with a lid containing tea. At first, your subject will be awkwardly startled and not know what to think. It will not taste like coffee, nor will it taste like tea right away.

In the world of behavioral economics, this is formulated by the fathers of *prospect theory*, Kahnemann and Tversky (1979) as "our perceptual apparatus is attuned to the evaluation of changes rather than to the evaluation of absolute magnitude [...] an object at a given temperature may be experienced as hot or cold to the touch depending on the temperature to which one had adapted." Likewise, if you expect to make a million dollars going into your salary negotiation, you are—at least most of us would be—guaranteed to come out unhappy, feeling that you have just lost $970K (if you are the average American worker) instead of being happy about the $30K you have been offered. This $30k is still way better than the nothing you make while unemployed. This is a little bit the glass half-full versus half-empty meme.

So expect low, while aiming high in negotiations. This will offer you the most happiness you can get, while it will still prime the other party to pay you more than they initially intended.

2. Building the Best Expectation
In an upscale New York French gourmet restaurant at a special event, Tuscani pasta was served. Afterwards customers were asked for their opinions. Tuscani got the most favorable ratings from the diners. When they were told that they were in fact served Pizza Hut's new pasta creation, they were in disbelief.

Our mind builds expectations; and whatever we see, feel, or get helps us to reinforce, intensify, and strengthen these expectations. The event will then be mainly experienced based on the expectation rather than by its actual characteristics. The ad campaign for a perfume or a purse is therefore a central part in the value that you purchase and consume. If you are told and believe something will be good or bad, chances are that you will perceive it as such. This is called the *expectation bias*. Check out the following examples as well:
• Coffee places with upscale ambience simply make coffee taste better. That is part of the reason

Starbucks coffee tastes much better than Dunkin' Donuts for many of us, while blind tasting might reveal different results.

- Remember the famous Pepsi challenge on TV in the '80s? Even though people prefer Pepsi's taste, they largely buy Coke. This is because we do not primarily buy a well-tasting beverage—we buy a feeling. So Coke in a Coke can tastes different because we expect different.
- Based on this presumption, we can even be fooled into enjoying bad stuff. In a study, Dan Ariely gave subjects beer with vinegar and regular beer to rate. Those expecting real beer rated it exactly like real beer.

Apparently, taste is not about the quality of the food or whether freshly prepared pasta is healthier than its canned brother, but about your expectation and subsequent realization of joy. As you see, your expectations will influence how much you will like it. In the end, how much you like it is an indicator for your willingness to pay.

A top lawyer can ask for top money because you expect top service, and when you listen to his advice, you will most likely perceive it as such. What can you learn? Be critical! Even a top lawyer or a top whatever makes mistakes or coasts on his or her reputation. A star usually has reasons that allowed her to build up that reputation, but they must not necessarily help your specific cause. In my business career, I always liked to work with people who were up-and-coming because I know they are eager to succeed, willing to put in the extra mile, and cheaper.

Another famous application of this reality distortion are placebo pills. Those pills do not contain any active ingredients, yet patients are told they work. Countless studies have made them a proven cheap and effective cure for many diseases. Sometimes just seeing a doctor helps start the healing process. The doctor does not even have to prescribe any medication. In consequence, you might wonder, why should we not be able to heal ourselves in many cases? After all, our body was built, i.e., grown without any external help too.

A placebo 2.0 experiment was conducted with headache pills. They all contained the same amount of active ingredients but were sold at different prices. The results indicated that more expensive pills work better. If the subject had experience with painkillers, the effect was even stronger. They did not need more or stronger medication but a more expensive one — unknowingly of the same type — to feel relief. Exactly the same was found for energy drinks. High-priced, highly advertised drinks apparently make the average consumer perform better. A cheap energy drink does not work as well, even if it has the same liquid in the can as one study tried with SoBe. That probably means that Red Bull can make you fly if you just expect it enough. Taken to the extreme, on the other end, this also means that good clear water can do the same for you. Maybe you have heard of the belief in artesian spring water and its powers. This is water that rises by itself from a natural ground-level source. Conveniently, regular water has the same chemical compound H2O and contains similar minerals. Therefore, the result should be equivalent. All you need is to believe. You can be smarter, more awake, just by drinking water.

So after you have read and fully digested this, most energy drinks should not have an effect much different from that of water on you anymore. Most generic medicines can now work just as well for you. You do not need the advertisement for a product to be great. Build expectations by yourself for yourself and you can enjoy a no-name product just like a branded one.

Learn how to decouple your expectation from the public image some items or places have and you can find priceless joy in life. An extreme example is my great-aunt. She recently passed after one of the happiest yet poor peasant lives in her early '90s. Her entire life she spent on her small farm, and she took so much pride in her few possessions — simple clothes and humble furniture. She even had a car seat in her kitchen for years. When she would tell you about her belongings, you could imagine her living in a palace with fine drapes at the walls, the latest lingerie, and design furniture. She was proud, genuinely happy, and you would not feel any dishonesty, self-mockery, or deceit in her words. She was happy, believed she was happy, expected to be happy with what she had, and in turn, she was happy. While she did not understand why she was happy, she never asked either. If she had started asking herself, she might have endangered that deep inner sense of happiness. So for her it was a good thing she never asked as she did not have the tools and understanding to investigate. But we can learn from her and knowingly expect happiness from our lives and from the things we buy. As Andre Agassi's coach Brad Gilbert used to say, "Good stuff will happen." And good stuff happened.

3. Making It the Best Experience

How do you consume? In order to attain a certain feeling, you will need a certain input. However, different causes have varying kinds of effects. For instance, we need 1.7 times more sugar in a watery soft drink to double our perception of sweetness. So this is pretty cheap as returns increase faster than the input. But there are many other consumables with diminishing returns – i.e., less effect for each additional unit of input. Therefore, eating a piece of chocolate on five separate occasions during the day will be more enjoyable than eating a whole bar at once.

Let's look at something more irrational. Ultimately, the current moment is just a vanishing sliver of time compared to the ever-growing memories of our past. So how do we get a truly great, memorable experience? It needs to have a high intensity of positive emotions and an amazing ending. The duration is almost negligible. This holds true for bad experiences in the inverse as well. Consider two scenarios:

A. Your hand is fully immersed in painfully cold water for one minute.
B. Your hand is fully immersed in painfully cold water for one minute and subsequently immersed in slightly less cold water for 30 seconds.

Which experience would you prefer? While I am sure you would instantaneously say A, test subjects actually replied in unison that B was much better after trying. This is the effect of the improved ending mentioned above.

In this context, Dan Ariely had once unwillingly conducted a personal pain experiment. While he was terribly injured and burned as an assassination collateral victim in Israel, he found that the long, continuous pain produced by slowly removing his bandages was much more agreeable than repeated short intense pains of bandages being ripped off his body. The sum of the stimuli was the same as it was the same set of bandages every time, but the less he could get used to it, the more intense the feelings were. This is another example where the peak intensity is the only relevant factor in what we remember.

Freedom Looming over the Horizon

This sounds like a lot to go through? Initially, it will seem like a strange process. As time goes by, this will become very natural and your mind will open and volunteer the right thoughts without much effort.

The way you contemplate while making your decision also influences the outcome. Therefore, while you ponder, envision the freedom and beauty of life without the item instead of imagining owning the item. As we have seen, creating an ownership emotion is a tricky issue that leads to overpayments.

In the end, after you have fulfilled your desire and saved some money, consciously enjoy the thought that you have what you want and a little more. Now you have some money you could use to fulfill another dream another day. So keep it and rejoice in the thought of the freedom you have just earned yourself.

Key Points to Remember

- Our motivations can be grouped into five categories — i.e., physiological, safety, love/belonging, esteem, and self-actualization. The order of their fulfillment impacts the overall quality of our satisfaction.

- Think of ways to help yourself make better choices: positive procrastination, ownership versus usage, evaluate alternatives, right size, configure to the minimum, reuse creatively.

- *Defaulting*: When things get complicated, your mind will pick the default option. But the defaults can greatly differ depending on your perspective. So play through a few scenarios until you know what is right.

- When making up your mind, beware of the *opportunity cost*. It is not worth spending more time on the decision than you are potentially saving.

- Some alternative might become unavailable if you wait too long. Remember that girl that got together with another guy for good while you couldn't make up your mind? However, scarcity is scarce in today's economy. Instead, other things get cheaper over time, so waiting might occasionally be a good idea.

- Carefully consider where to buy. Prices vary among stores, channels, and geographies.

- According to *prospect theory*, we focus on changes rather than on absolute magnitudes. This has three interesting implications:

- We tend to only see the difference between expectation and fact. So expect low while aiming high.

- We usually get what we expect, as we often refuse to realize and accept any difference between expected and real outcome (*expectation bias*).

- We can even change the way we experience fact to further meet our expectation. For instance, by using the fact that peak intensity is the only relevant factor in what we remember.

Attraction

"Sweet coupled airs we sing.
No lonely seafarer
Holds clear of entering
Our green mirror."
—Homer
Ancient Greek poet
The Siren's call from *The Odyssey*

"Attraction is beyond our will or ideas sometimes."
—Juliette Binoche
French actress

When it comes to commerce, we have to deal not only with the product or service at hand but also with the setting it is being sold in, the advertisement strategy used to promote it, and eventually the salespeople pushing the product or helping us navigate the marketplace. They all divert us from our previously discussed ambition.

After looking at the elements that constitute the marketplace, the ensuing chapters are designed as your guidebook against the commercial magic of the 21st century. They will show a number of attraction strategies used by businesses to persuade us into buying. These can occur in any form or shape and apply to one or more elements of the marketplace. We will, however, not discuss pricing at this point as it deserves its own chapter due to its broad implications.

Would you want to start with a little exercise? Take some of your favorite food that does not spoil quickly and put it in an open container right in front of you. Maybe some chocolate, gummy bears, or beef jerky — whatever it is you really enjoy. Now keep reading this book or doing whatever you are doing without giving in to the tempting food. How long can you last?

I won't blame you if you finish the food pretty soon. So here are two tricks: To help you keep your distance, first, associate a happy feeling with not eating it. Visualize how great you feel without it, and as you do so, do not picture the food in your mind. Second, simply keep open or easily accessible food out of your vicinity. Even a wrapped sandwich in your line of sight will be eaten. So keep your lunch in your bag or in a place farther out of range, especially if it is something you could smell.

Attraction is all around us.

Constituents of the Marketplace

As you will see, we live in a more or less scripted lab experiment. Companies spend billions of dollars to learn about the consumer animal. The more they know about the other market participants, the more advantageous their position will be. I will show you that we are sometimes more influenced by what some clever strategists want us to buy than by our own free will. Should there be a moral question mark? Critics, as

Thomas Sattelberger, chief HR officer at Deutsche Telekom AG, consider behavioral economics "morally rotten". The proponents are saying that everything is fine since after they make us want it, we actually want it. By then, it is our true desire.

The Product/Service Itself

A misty summer day in downtown San Francisco, I was invited to visit the offices of Frog Design Inc., a German-founded now California-based creative powerhouse. Stepping out of the elevator, I saw tons of Apple products. Unfamiliar ones. Products that had never seen the light of day. Apparently, they had helped come up with Apple's landmark design. It is their specialty to design products that make us instantly fall in love with them. One of the things I learned there was that round corners make us subconsciously like the product more.

The Setting

Do you love Apple Stores? The well-lit, spacious environment? What could be more conducive to sales? According to Gartner, Apple turns its inventory every 5 days, ranking it only behind McDonalds'. Dell takes about 10 days, and Samsung 21. Well-lit is big for sales. You might have noticed that even many gas stations have become much friendlier-looking than they used to be 20 years ago.

At the example of retailers, I will show you a few more ways the store setup can tempt us. For years supermarkets have simply placed margin-strong products on eye level, but this game has just been stepped up. Supermarkets are not just arbitrarily arranged aisles with product shelves. Instead, they are designed based on experience and experiments with people wearing GPS-like units or even mobile EEGs (brain activity monitors) walking through aisles of test markets. New market layouts are tried out in stunningly authentic-feeling virtual reality simulators.

One interesting finding is that we buy more walking counterclockwise through a market, $2 more on average per store visit, that is. What is your home supermarket's setup like?

Also, with an average visit to a store, we cover only about 25% of the market; so some places like IKEA will force us to pretty much walk the entire store before we make it to the cashier.

Since we usually tend to spend most of our time on the perimeter of the market, we just dash into the aisles where we are expecting to find a product we are looking for. Therefore, sales on the ends of the aisles are much higher than in the center of the aisles. That is why you will find products with better margins for the supermarket at the ends and in end-cap displays. According to Bart Weitz, executive director of the University of Florida's Center for Retailing Education and Research, putting an item on an end-cap of a supermarket aisle can boost sales by 300%. Best value for money, on the contrary, is at the less frequented places in the middle of the aisles. Next time you notice a "good deal," remember that because you noticed it, it is probably a staged deal primarily good for the vendor. The good deals for you are typically somewhat hidden.

In the near future, you will see supermarkets roll out black shelves and LED lighting in the dairy section. Pilots have been run in Spain and France. Danone has found in studies that these can substantially increase sales in this category because it makes us feel warmer and more comfortable. The more time we spend, the more money we leave.

Lines waiting at the cashier are a huge facilitator for sales. Studies by the IHL Consulting Group have shown a 43% decline in sales of candy, gum, and breath mints, 53% lower sales of chips and salty snacks, and 50% drop in soda and water when they compared old-fashioned cashiers stuffed with product displays to self-checkout counters. With the new chore of checking out ourselves, we are just too busy with the process to pay attention to anything else. This is an easy way to save us from buying stuff we really do not need. It might even help you lose some weight. "On average, we believe that self-checkout will save somebody two-and-a-half-pounds a year," said Greg Buzek, president of IHL. Furthermore, using the self-checkout also inflicts some pain of paying on you with the associated benefits as we discussed earlier in this book. Despite all the benefits of checking out yourself, remember that it will usually take you longer to do it on your own.

Advertisement Strategies

A recent trip led me to NeuroFocus Inc., a company based in Berkeley, California, and according to its website "the world's largest neuromarketing research firm, leveraging breakthrough neuroscience advances for business and market research."[5] So what are these advances? I was invited into a room where study participants wearing EEGs were watching commercials for a well-respected credit card company. Bundles of cables as thick as arms protruded from the participants' heads into NeuroFocus's servers in much of a sci-fi fashion. Based on the observed brain waves,

---

[5] www.neurofocus.com, as of May 17, 2012.

a proprietary algorithm automatically rates every instant of the commercial and cuts it to a spot of desired length, say 30 seconds instead of a minute, and only leaves the most powerful parts in. The resulting commercial is not only much cheaper to air but also considerably more effective, evoking a lightning storm in your head by firing synapses that make you want that card. It really works, and it is 100% automated. In numbers, that means by putting down a six-figure fee, they can now save a 7+ figure airtime fee and get a better turnout. Amazing, isn't it? That is not an exception anymore. It is becoming the rule.

NeuroFocus was also in the process of launching a wireless EEG device that I can say was very comfortable to wear. This wireless device allows monitoring consumer reactions in their environments. Whether at home or at a supermarket shelf. Ever wondered how you feel while taking that Coke out of your fridge? You might never know, but Coke soon will for sure. If you are at a large retailer or buying a mass market product, you can be sure that it was engineered to be desired or designed to channel your desires toward high-margin products.

While the above is still an undifferentiated approach, technological advances allow for an increasing amount of targeted advertising. Direct mailings based on data mining were an early stage. So for today's state of the art, why not take a moment and go to http://www.google.com/ads/preferences. This is Google's settings page for Google Ads that are shown on your computer. I never knew about it until I interviewed a Google employee in late 2011. Apparently, the page is not widely promoted. My Google resume, as I will call it, told me that I was aged

30 to 35 and interested in spots cars and behavioral economics and a few more things we will not discuss here. When I checked again at the time of publication, Google seemed to have changed this to an opt-in process, but it still worked. Try it for a couple of weeks and you will be surprised what Google knows about you just from your surfing behavior. This knowledge is used to change the search results to make them more specific and to present more relevant ads to you. The same applies to Facebook, which pretty much knows everything about us by now since most sites have "Like" buttons. When I go to a site about Buenos Aires, I will see ads by Lufthansa. Google knows my favorite airline and concludes that I am much more likely to actually make a reservation with them than with any other airline, so why post ads in vain? Then I have a Mac, so I do not see ads for PC software anymore.

While there are certainly benefits to this, it also means that the Internet is filtered. We only get to see what some algorithms think we need to see, whether it is ads or content. In turn, we might miss out on the special offers from the Cadillac dealer because some software thought we would not be interested or — worse — estimates we have enough money and should pay full price.

Most offers you see online are primarily beneficial to the other party yet seem attractive to you. There is hardly a way to get around it, except being aware, keeping your eyes open, and surfing with a second browser in total privacy mode through a VPN that provides you with a different IP.

Salespeople — Guides and Seducers
A good salesperson's passion is selling, mainly selling himself — no matter what the actual product or

service at stake is. We often see them as guides to navigate the confusing marketplace. Yet oftentimes, all they do is seduce us into something we do not need or cannot afford.

Some say business is war. That is in line with Sun Tzu's *The Art of War* being one of the management bibles of the last century. It is actually an ancient collection of Chinese war stratagems. Good news, sales has become less offensive in recent history. Overly pushy sales techniques have been discounted. More subtle techniques are on the rise. Edward de Bono has written a wonderful work on how to make yourself liked and accepted by others. Such tactics are the foundation to build the partnerships and establish the win-wins that are taught as the new mantra today. Despite win-win, salespeople still usually earn commission on their sales, and companies' profits directly depend on how much value they can extract from the consumers, from us.

The opportunities for win-win in your daily purchasing are pretty limited. Where do you win because Walmart makes more money? Well, they might invest more in your local store and expand it so you can buy even more. However, in other cases — especially with larger tickets — there are truly win-win outcomes possible.

We need to understand what is going on so we can fight for our win in win-win.

A carnivore and a passionate cook, I love to invite friends over for dinner. For years I have been preparing chili dinners almost every month. How much ground beef do you need for chili to feed 10 friends? I would say, I have pretty good handle on that, but if I ask my butcher — any butcher I have tried this with—for ground beef for 10, he will easily oversell me by 25–30%.

The same pretty much every time I ask for a quarter-pound cured ham, for instance, I hear, "Do you mind if it is a little more?" Yes, I do. Especially if the little turns out to be almost another quarter pound. Consistently employing this strategy can easily increase sales by 10% or more. If you feel bad for saying no to your sweetheart butcher, why not simply ask for an ounce less than you actually want? He will take good care of you with the extra ounce. And you will pay for that extra ounce. So it is all fair.

Many small-business salespeople play this game on a spontaneous basis—possibly they have some heuristics in their heads—whether they know about it or not. Yet larger institutions cluster their customers according to certain features to derive standard courses of action for the salespeople. That makes training easier and ensures a more consistent customer experience. Even such down-to-earth institutions as the Hamburger Sparkasse (Hamburg, Germany, Savings and Loan) create psycho profiles of its customers to help salespeople pick ideal approaches.

Businesses that sell complex products put significant effort into training their salespeople for ideal behavior. There are even studies how to mention a price for it to be more effective in a sales conversation. Nothing is left to chance. Or as Louis Pasteur said, "Chance favors the prepared mind." It is your choice to be at least as prepared, too.

Edward de Bono's Beautiful Mind

In his book *How to Have a Beautiful Mind*, Nobel Prize nominee Edward de Bono makes the point that attractiveness does not depend on physical features but almost entirely relies on having a fascinating, creative, and exciting mind.

He clearly illustrates that the beautiful mind is about imagination and using your creativity. Being highly educated or intelligent is not a prerequisite. True beauty comes from within. Accordingly, he offers a workout for the mind, explaining such seemingly simple things as various ways to agree and disagree. Ultimately, his teachings show ways to become a truly interesting person that draws people into memorable conversations.

This is yet again a book that has transformed my life, allowing me to win over people to my causes that would previously not even have looked at me.

Attractive Motives

Caveman Principle

We were hunters and gatherers for most of our 200,000-year history. Our recent antecedents were roaming the savannas of Africa. This is the reason that exactly this behavior is hardwired into our brains. Throughout the bigger part of history, things were scarce and perishable. There was not much we could actually collect and keep. Scarcity further drove the perceived preciousness of property and eventually led to the ownership bias. However, the world has changed. It has become increasingly easy to amass property. Yet today there is an ever increasing burden of maintaining all what we carry through our lives. In a desperate move, George Clooney in *Up in the Air* teaches how to fit your entire life into a rucksack. Well, as the movie succinctly points out, that did not work for him either. We cannot just go back. But the minimum lifestyle, as discussed a few chapters before, provides some good inspiration nonetheless.

Image Effect

In more or less conscious ways, we want to be a specific person. We have an idea in mind of how we would like to be perceived. And we act on that. We choose based on the reflections our decisions have on our image. That's image motivation or the image effect. You do not believe it? When you go out with friends, what do they order? What do you order?

Consider this example: There are two groups of people, the conformist and the nonconformist. Dan Ariely has shown in his famous beer study that people tend to be more on the former side. He had a brew pub offer a selection of new beers to groups, and the results showed that the first person's choice highly influenced all the others. In a setting where orders had to be written down individually and handed over to the server, the variance of beers ordered was significantly higher. It was concluded that we try to please our friends by showing that we are part of the same group, and that effect gets pretty strong once a few individuals have all made the same choice, even if you would actually feel like another brand of beer. Consequently, this effect leads to higher complexity in restaurants where you order in writing such as Bagger Dave's or fast-food joints where you order in a line but can't always overhear other orders. Regular seated dining has the highest conformity levels.

These motivations also force people to make knowingly wrong decisions, such as when solving simple math problems. In another study, several conspirators of the researcher had answered a given problem with a previously agreed wrong solution. Subsequently, the actual subject also chose the wrong solution and even admitted to knowing better during the debriefing. And we are talking about simple math problems that the control group solved perfectly and no beer involved this time. Imagine what this means for more complex group dynamics.

On the other side, the nonconformist confidently choses something different from the group.

What type are you? Next time you are in a bar and someone forces a drink on you, think about whether you are thirsty or confident enough not to please. Only drinking when I want has saved me thousands of dollars and countless headaches over the years. It can even earn you compliments on your strong sense of confidence — although those are quite rare.

What car do you drive? Ramit Sethi proudly confides that he — as most other Indians — drives a boring four-door sedan like a Toyota Camry or a Honda Accord. He does not waste his money on status cars like highly priced roadsters. He places more value on practical utility, which at the same time probably allows him to be mobile for half the money that I spend. The status symbol does not matter to him.

When talking about status symbols, there comes a time when it is not only about you anymore. Once you have a family, you represent more than yourself. You also represent your family, and your wife and kids might have very different ideas on what your family should stand for. So I am curious to see if Ramit will keep his Camry for life. The need for status symbols is very deeply rooted in our society.

As it is deeply ingrained in our psyche, this effect is so strong and difficult to overcome. We are concerned about what we portray not only to people around us but also to imaginary supervisors. Have you ever seen donation boxes with a photograph of someone staring at you atop? Or is there one of these photos next to the honesty box at your office's candy station? If so, this is no coincidence. A study has shown that when someone is watching us — even just a photograph — we are three times more likely to pay for the candy bar we take and we also donate noticeably more. This shows you how deeply rooted the image motives are. Once you have called the cheat, it will be your turn to make the game.

In a similar fashion, this was used to drive down crime. A few years back when gas prices were skyrocketing, more and more people were filling up their cars and then just drove off. So gas stations in Michigan put up pictures next to the pumps. They were showing a cop intensely staring at you with his arms crossed and a strict warning that you would go to jail if...

Lastly, image motivation also works in the reverse by barring you from doing certain things. In the past, it has saved us from many dubious expenses. Asking for a porn magazine at a gas station counter was a hurdle for most of us. Today, people download all sorts of stuff with little to no monetary cost online. Credit card statements only show anonymous merchants spouses cannot identify. Without noticing, large chunks of time go wasted. So if you want to overcome your porn addiction, why not put a framed photograph of your spouse or mother next to your computer?

Loyalty

Almost 50% of Toyota costumers have owned a Toyota before. But despite a plethora of brands available, they have chosen Toyota again. The same applies for GM, Ford, and other makes. Why? Deep inside we are loyal. Whether it is our car or the little mom-and-pop store at the corner, where we feel like we have to go and buy something once in a while, we are loyal to brands just as we are loyal to people. That is already a good buying motivator. Companies have realized that and build on our loyalty, trying to expand it.

Loyalty is rewarded. Businesses know we love to get hooked. By giving us a little something extraordinary in return, they cater to our social needs and make us feel special. It works by making our body release dopamine, which induces happiness and at the same time makes us addicted to more of its cause. In a world that is increasingly deprived of real social contacts like ours, the effects are all the stronger.

While I was living in Nashville, I frequently enjoyed the Regal Movie Theater. As I learned about great deals for holders of their free loyalty card, I signed up. The card offered regular rewards, such as free drinks and free movie tickets every so many visits. Well, truth be told, before that, I went to the movies once a quarter, but during that time in Nashville, I literally saw every single movie that was released except *The Texas Chainsaw Massacre*. The revenue the theater extracted out of me and my friends more than tripled despite the freebies. Profits soared! Furthermore, I have not set foot into any other theater in the Nashville area. While this was extreme—I like living on the edge as you might have figured by now—

it illustrates the point that those companies have figured out. Loyalty programs make us spend much more. Considering the *decreasing utility of each additional unit* we consume, we could spend our money elsewhere and get better returns. Ask yourself, just how much happier do you get from going to the theater five instead of three times a month?

At most times, we cannot afford to be "loyal" to more than one. That is also the reason in most societies men can only marry one woman instead of multiple, and if they can marry multiple times, such as in Islam, this is strictly regulated to ensure equal treatment of all wives.

In my case, I have airline memberships for Star Alliance, SkyTeam, and OneWorld. As with the ladies, despite flying a distance equivalent of several times around the globe in some years, I can only be loyal to one. For the others, I do not even collect miles as they typically expire before I have accumulated enough to get an award. Since most destinations are served by multiple carriers, I mostly have a clear airline preference. That is good for the airline, and I know: otherwise, the airline would not be as "loyal" to me either.

This leads to some borderline insane behavior: When you read online forums for frequent fliers, you will find people exchanging strange strategies to earn more miles. They fly less convenient routes to earn more miles. Or they buy higher-priced tickets just to get more miles. Lufthansa, for instance, offers tickets with half the miles, regular miles, and double miles within the economy booking class. Really. Or mile hunters fly to South Africa for Christmas to add some miles before the year-end counter reset.

While all the neatly colored plastics in your wallet are a strong source for image effects, and loyalty feels like the right thing, think again how much value you can derive from an airport lounge and the other amenities. Basically, there are the following things offered with airline clubs. If you really fly a lot, you will get access and enjoy it. That is true and fair. If you do not fly so much, ask yourself about the true value of the club you aspire.

Benefit	Value
lounge access	Only very few airlines actually provide quality food — Lufthansa is one of them. How much would you pay to buy comparable food at the airport? How much are you paying to get into the club in time and additional fares? If you really need lounge access, get an Amex Platinum or simply buy your way in for an average of $45 as some US airlines allow. Okay, Lufthansa will not let you in if you are not a member, but really, it is not that great either. If you are still not convinced, let me tell you that I had to sit on the floor on several occasions — even in first-class lounges of some US carriers — as they were overcrowded.
priority at security	Skip lines at the airport by confidence. That will work too, and

	saves time and money.
priority boarding	This is only relevant if you want to bring a lot of luggage on board. Otherwise you actually want to board last to save yourself some valuable time. Airlines, however, promote early boarding as it ensures timely or even early departures, which in turn lowers airport fees.
luggage priority handling	This is probably the only thing that is worth it if you fly economy and check your luggage. It is included with higher classes anyway, and without it, waiting for your luggage is just painful. But waiting a few times for your luggage is still less time than taking an extra stop in Houston on your way from Vancouver to new NYC to earn extra miles.
cheaper loyalty flights	Ask yourself, are the cheaper flights really cheaper if you pay more in unnecessary fares for flights to get access to them?
status card	Do you need to show off to your peers how much you fly? How often do they even see your plastic?

To sum up, if you are at least a somewhat regular traveler, you still want to be a member of these loyalty programs and reap as many benefits as you can. But consolidate to make sure you actually get enough points or miles to actually earn awards. Other than a generic credit card, you could go for an airline credit card that collects miles for your favorite carrier with every purchase. In a second step, link all your hotel reward programs to one airline. For instance, I collect Lufthansa Miles on my Intercontinental Hotel Groups Priority Pass and on my T-Mobile Phone bill. That way, I never face the situation that I do not have enough miles to fly, not enough points for a hotel room, and some useless points in some other scheme that I do not even understand. It also saves me the hassle of keeping track of all the accounts, as they expire and so on.

Our Own Moods

Do you know the YouTube Channel "Bad Day? Go Shopping!!" by ShoppaHolicGiiirly? Moods impact our purchasing desires and decisions. They make us susceptible to things we would otherwise easily forgo or not even consider. Marketers have found out about this and try to benefit.

Research has shown that we compensate for negative moods by shopping and that we also shop to complement positive ones. This is especially true for apparel as the above anecdotal evidence illustrates. In fact, the research even concludes that moods might well be the primary driver for shopping and thus a key lever for you to work on.

Interestingly, moods can also drive us toward more experiential goods. People primed with an awe-inducing experience show a tendency toward them. Material desires are pushed back.

As our moods are determined by the way we feel, the experiences we had and are having, as well as what is happening around us, sellers try to adjust our environment to create the ideal shopping moods. Since this is not always easy, there is the less elaborate method of simply positioning products toward certain moods.

My personal favorite is the German chocolate bar pictured here. We are being conditioned to have some chocolate every time we feel bad and we will feel better. However, our threshold of needing a chocolate fix is lowered each time. Mood-driven consumption facilitates further consumption in the future. This has negative long-term effects on mental and physical health. The result is emotional addiction.

Source: "Solace Chocolate", own picture

As we see, moods are dangerous fellows. Once we consciously think about it, spending money for something useless may provide short-term satisfaction;

however, it ultimately leaves us poorer and more deprived of what we really want.

Now that we are aware of the mood addiction, how can we free ourselves from it? The easiest way would be a Barney Stinson-type state control: "When I feel sad, I stop being sad and be awesome instead. True story." This character from the TV show *How I Met Your Mother* can pretty much change his mood in the blink of an eye or at least make you believe he can. Even though you can actually learn to do this to a certain degree, you will always be in some mood. And each mood will drive a certain behavior.

So what you will really want to do is work on the link between mood and behavior. You can use the "Mood Behavior Matrix" provided in the supporting material. While in a calm, unaroused state — maybe after getting up one morning — make a list of your main moods. Add three more columns. Once you are done, write next to each mood what type of habits you fall into when in that one. For instance, sadness might lead you to eat ice cream, joy might make you call your friends and not stop talking (which might annoy them) and so on. In the third column, note what healthy activity you would rather like to fall into. When you are sad, you could go kickboxing. When you are joyful, you could start sharing your joy by complimenting people around you. It can be anything. The forth column is your space to put down a few steps of how you can make this change as easy as possible — almost automatic. Maybe you will need to sign up for that kickboxing gym first; maybe you need to buy some new running gear. Then put that list into your wallet or somewhere where you see it several times a day. And next time your mood changes to one of the listed ones, go do your new thing. You will see after a few times your habit will have changed.

	Current Behavior	Aspired Behavior	Facilitating Steps
Sadness	Eat ice-cream	Go kickboxing	Have my sports bag ready at all times. Have my sports bag in the car. ...
Joy	Talk too much	Compliment others	Make a list of things to look for in other people that can easily be complimented.

Attractive Values

Not everything in commerce is superficial bling. Actually we are quite invested in our values. We like it when they are shared. Businesses know that, so they promote certain ones believed to be shared by their target audience.

So whenever you see a salesperson matching your values, it is time to ask, whether it is for real, or whether he is trying to ease you into a sale? You can make some conclusions about this based on the values that you have demonstrated so far. If in doubt, try representing a false value as a trap and, once he supports it, disagree with him. Not only will you see how much he sticks to his value set but also will you possibly be able to force him into a concession.

Ads are value appeals. One of my values is boldness. Therefore, I enjoy bold ads and tend to gravitate toward the promoted products. Knowing this, when watching an interesting ad or before buying something in general, I ask myself why I like the product. On one hand, I might conclude that I was just enticed by the boldness and let go. On the other hand, I might still decide to buy the product to show off my value preference to my friends. And that is OK. It is just a different type of need, and it only takes so many bold products for me to do that sufficiently — if I do it conscientiously.

A common value is simplicity. Bad news, life is not simple. We love heuristics, ways of finding a quick and easy decision in an overwhelmingly complicated environment. I just picked up a brochure that advertised retirement plans. On page 5 there was a quick test. In eight questions, I could determine the ideal plan. Tempting, for sure. But can an issue complicated as an investment with a 50-year horizon really be solved with eight yes/no questions? We want to believe it could. But it cannot. You will pay the price for this simplicity eventually.

In general, Americans tend to be optimists, individualists, and *outlaws at heart*. So expect a lot of ads into that direction. Think of the 2012 Super Bowl commercials. I have just checked the top 10, and there was not even a single one that did not allude to at least one of those values.

There is the other side of values too. We might be missing good opportunities because the product does not appeal to our values. It might be a foreign product or intended for a different generation. How far you are willing to go is your call. Think: blue Jeans made in North Korea.

Visual Attraction

Now, let me take you to the other end of the tangibility spectrum with a look at colors, images, and movies.

Color

Does it matter in which color a product is presented to you? What color a salesperson wears?

Primates are the only mammals that can see red. Millions of years ago, at some point we started to develop red vision as it helped us distinguish ripe fruits, fresh meats, and poisonous animals. It served us well. Red spikes testosterone release in men and increases aggressiveness. More about sexual heat later. Today among all colors, red is still the color we notice first. That is why not only many company logos are red, but also signs posted in supermarkets and on roadways (including traffic lights). Yes, it is true that the only participants at bullfights actually seeing red are the torero and the spectators. The poor bull is just intrigued by the funny moves, the crowd, and oftentimes some other measures that are truly questionable in regard to animal rights.

Another exciting color is blue as it makes us trusting. Salespeople dressed in blue or presentations with a blue background make us produce oxytocin, a trust hormone. We cannot help it. So if you want to be sure she says yes, propose under the blue sky wearing a blue shirt and jeans.

I leave it up to the reader to make up his mind what this color rating means for American politics.

In addition to our genetic reception of colors, an acquired sense for colors is defined very early in life. Remember your old Fisher-Price toys? Now, have a look at *USA Today* and the original iMac or iPhone icons. Notice anything? The color scheme is pretty much the same. With those colors, the products evoke feelings of childhood happiness. And happiness we seek.

Images

There are tons of images and pictures around us every day. Ask yourself, would your willingness to spend change if the website selling a product had dollar signs in the background? In a study, 86% of people said that while remembering the wallpaper of the website, it had not influenced their purchasing behavior. Yet it had. That is a stark lack of awareness. So next time you see coins pictured or dollar signs, remember that this influences us to look for bargains. Most people will walk out of that store with the cheapest option. You don't buy a $300 all-round barbecue set at a dollar store. Note that another background could also invoke a motive of quality, and you will seek just that.

Here is one for the male readership: Sorry, guys, sex sells and we buy. The spirit might often be willing, but the flesh is weak. So we give in to temptation. A study with a South African bank showed that men increase their borrowing to the same extent as they would have with a 25% drop in interest rates if the advertisement included the picture of a woman. And that woman was just a stock picture headshot with a businesslike attire. No tits anywhere. Obviously, there was no effect on women. A different setup using a picture of a man did not have an impact on either sex.

The reasons behind this are not entirely clear; however, one possible explanation is that men typically chase after women. They have fewer mating opportunities, so they risk more by attempting to gain the favor of women. Women, on the other hand, pretty much block out unwanted or unworthy prospective sexual partners.

Next time you see a woman's face on a sign-up form, think twice before hitting Submit.

Movies

It only gets more intense with motion pictures. We have discussed the manipulative design of TV commercials. Additionally, as you might have known, the volume of commercials is always a little louder than the surrounding programming. This is done to catch your attention. So if you cannot skip it, mute it. Germany has chosen to enforce normalized volume across channels and during shows as of September 2012. For my case, that will be too late—I have even gone as far as to completely ban the TV from my life. If I want to watch my favorite weekly show; I do so online on CBS.com for free (some commercials) or on iTunes. And for movies, there is Netflix. No cable or dish can ever compete with its hassle-free $7 a month.

How subversive can it get? A study has shown that if we are flashed a picture for just 1/25 of a second during every second, we will be influenced even though the sequence is below the threshold of being noticeable. In an experiment, thirsty volunteers exposed to such short flashes of smiling faces were willing to pay up to three times the price for a subsequently offered drink than those shown grimaces.

Do not watch if you do not trust the source. But is this really an option?

Verbal Attraction

"The pen is mightier than the sword," English author Edward Bulwer-Lytton stated in 1839. Well today, words and the ways they are presented to us make all the difference in how we behave.

Words

Advertising tells us many things. It might not be outright lies, but they are certainly not fully true either. Do you believe what you see on TV? Or read on the Internet? Generally, you are a trusting person?

Have a look at cheaptickets.com. As of this writing, there are 65 references to the word *cheap* on the start page. Even though we know that they probably do not always have the cheapest fare, we somehow believe. In fact, they do not even list the typical low-cost airlines. And because it is so difficult to find the lowest overall fare with all the extra frills, like baggage fees and in-flight entertainment, we happily trust a website. Again when things get difficult, we always seek the shortcut instead of profoundly figuring it out. More about this in the section about forms below.

Have you ever read the sign "While supplies last"? It makes us want stuff. It is a proven fact that we buy more cans of soup if a sign says "Limit 12 per customer." In our modern economy, supplies hardly run dry, and if they really did, prices would surge first. So any sign like this is merely a trigger of some ancient caveman behavior meant to make us buy something we would not have bought otherwise.

Paraphrasing

How do you feel about a hair loss prevention treatment with a 30% success rate? Does not sound too bad. But what about one that is ineffective in 70% of all cases. Most people will happily buy the former and decline the latter. But they are effectively the same product with the same chances of success. Benedetto de Martino, of the University College London Institute of Neurology, points out, "It is well known that human choices are affected by the way in which a question is phrased. For example, saying an operation carries an 80 per cent survival rate may trigger a different response compared to saying that an operation has a 20 per cent chance of dying from it, even though they offer exactly the same degree of risk."[6] Next time a decision is presented to you, map it out. Do not look just at what is said, but also at what is not said. Then decide. Suddenly, a lot of products show a very different valuation.

Mail

E-mail newsletters take time to read. They take your attention away from more important things. Even worse, they actually make you buy things that you would not have wanted if you had not read about it. Remember that purse you never used, that new CD you never listened to? In fact right now, go to your e-mail folder and unsubscribe from everything from

---

[6] University College London (2006).

legitimate senders unless you truly need it. (Do not unsubscribe junk because that will only tell the sender that your address is valid and invite more spam.)

The same applies to your paper junk in your mailbox. Do not even look at it. I have a trashcan right next to the mailbox because I know once it is in the house, I will be tempted to read.

In the end, you will want to consider a media diet, just as Tim Ferriss suggests in his *The 4-Hour Workweek*. This is the only way to free hours every day for valuable pastimes. It also saves you a lot of money you would otherwise spend on media and other unnecessary desires.

Forms

I wonder when the first form in history was designed. If you know, please get in touch. Forms are such a great invention facilitating communication or making it more difficult. They are a fabulous way to steer behavior too. The designer has an amazing degree of control, whether you are talking about tax return forms, mail order forms, organ donation sign-ups, or anything else.

Let me give you a funny example. My mom just received a retirement claim validation request form the social security: a form of about 30 pages. One question read, "Have you been sick for at least one month between age 17 and 24?" I was visiting that day, and I could tell you we had a blast laughing about this. Sadly, however, this is an excellent method for them to deny or reduce claims as I am sure not everyone is willing or able to go through the ordeal of submitting this form.

On most forms, we find decisions that are either opt-in or opt-out. In general, we tend to leave it the way it is. Catalogs, for instance, often come with order forms where certain items are filled in already. We do not want them—ah, they are just $5. Maybe they are not so bad after all. So we leave them. How many people act this way? If only a few do, it is already worth trying for those companies.

Consider the following example regarding organ donation. When organ donation is the government mandated default and people have the right to opt out, 98%–100% stay organ donors. When you have to opt in to be one, only 0%–28% choose to be donors.

As briefly mentioned before, we refuse to make a choice, not only when the choice does barely matter but especially when it is difficult and complex. In those cases, we simply stick with the default. Therefore, let us call this *defaulting*. So while you have to be concerned about mail-order templates and newsletter subscriptions, you want to be even more vigilant about 401(k), health insurances, etc. When you got your last job, what packages did you pick? It might well be worth a second thought. The default is not always the best option for you, but most likely the best option for whoever created the form! Especially as setting up your 401(k) correctly is one of the most important financial foundations of your life. You will want to take that extra time.

Wildfires in Our Mind

The Prominent Feature Premium

Have you bought a laptop lately? You must have found a myriad of different configurations in the showroom. CPU frequency, memory size, hard disk type and space, graphical processors, and much more vary from model to model. How did you make your decision? What mattered to you? Some hard-to-define overall value of the laptop or a certain prominent feature like the CPU frequency?

Psychology professor Paul Slovic has conducted a simplified experiment to helps us understand how we compare several alternatives. He made subjects define pairs of alternatives of equal value. For instance, the following two packages of cash and a coupon book were identified as of equal total value:

- A: $10 cash and $32 coupon book value
- B: $20 cash and $18 coupon book value

At a later stage, everyone was asked to indicate what dimension (cash or coupons) was more important to them and to choose the package they preferred. Of course they should have been indifferent as initially defined, but 88% picked the package, which was stronger in the preferred dimension. So if you like coupons a lot, you would go for package 1 even though on a value basis both packages are the same to you.

Our choice is influenced by a prominent feature, and therefore, we are willing to pay a premium for it. Consequently, businesses drive our demand toward certain products by highly advertising specific features that are most likely important to us.

Back to the laptop: Maybe you know someone who bought one with a really strong CPU only to find out later that it was slow for its price because it lacked memory. Slovic found similar results in many domains, such as college applicants, tires, baseball players, and routes to work.

Takeaway: Know what you really want, and don't be influenced by a few prominent features that are likely to be placed to trap you.

Primed for Attraction

Have you ever heard a friend tell you about that new style that someone just pioneered and suddenly you see it all over? Every day you can recount several experiences of seeing it. It is ubiquitous. It feels like a new trend; you feel the pressure to get on it as well. There are just as many people wearing a different style, if not more, but nonetheless you almost feel like the last outsider.

Our perception can be infected by the virus of *priming*. I am liking it to an infection because once you catch it, it grows within you—unstoppable. Priming happens when you first hear or see something you were previously not conscious about. Then all of a sudden, you notice it everywhere. Priming defines the filter for your selective perception.

Your subconscious filters the plethora of impressions of the day and only allows for a few important stimuli to get to your consciousness. Once you are primed about something in particular, your subconscious deems this interesting to you and drops the appropriate filter. Then it shows you each occurrence of it.

This is the same effect that comes into play when you learn a new word and suddenly you hear everyone saying it—on TV, the radio, the Internet, and among your friends.

As a result of this, trendspotting is such a difficult endeavor. It is a conscious effort against the nature of your brain because we are hardwired to make patterns out of nothing, and consequently, we miss the real trends until they are way obvious.

The most popular manifestation of this effect is Friday the 13th—the unlucky day. We have been primed on Friday, October 13, 1307. Yes, that was more than 700 years ago. On that day, hundreds of Knights Templars were arrested by royal officials and the their prosperous realm brought to a sudden end.

Still today we are scared by the mere prospect of Friday the 13th.

Herding

When I was a kid, I once complained at the butchers that I always had to wait for my turn, no matter when I showed up. One day, the butcher lectured me. "If you run a store, it must never be empty, for if it is empty, people will think it is a bad store. So if there are only few customers, talk to them and make them stay as long as possible, and if there are plenty, speed up so they do not get too annoyed." Aha. He perfectly understood herding. We see other people who have made the decision presumably because it is a good butcher, so we line up too. Is it really a good butcher, or just a clever one?

Herding gets even more perverse when we consider self-herding (related to escalating commitment). Maybe one morning you think whether you really want to shave. After some consideration, you figure that it will not be a problem if you do not shave one day, especially since you are pressed for time anyway. Yet it has been a somewhat careful consideration. The next day, you wonder again. You remember you haven't shaved the last day, and it was good. So you line up behind yourself and skip shaving again. Before you notice, you stop consciously thinking about it, because you have made the decision in the past and found it to be good. You have grown a beard, built a habit. Believe me, I have done it and grown the most ugly beard you can imagine. I am still grateful to my friends who finally made me shave again.

This works just as well with eating chocolate, drinking beer regularly, buying useless trinkets, and much more. Once you are on a new habit, it only gets more intense. Like a spiral. Before you know it, there is hair growing out of your nose, you are drinking expensive imported beer, and you buy pseudo art for which you do not have a place. When you want to break a habit, you have to be conscious about this. Your life is full of habits, and the more you dig into it, the more arbitrary the initial decisions seem that have created them. It is never too late to challenge them.

Play, Touch, Sex

Here is to our favorite 3. No book without them. Not even this one.

Play

Today's big term in business is gamification—i.e., how can elements of play be added into serious products. If we can play, we enjoy using it more, we use it more, and we are more likely to buy it.

Source: https://www.facebook.com/cowclicker, Ian Bogost

The epitome and proof point is Cow Clicker, a Facebook-based nonsense game. All you can do here is own a virtual cow and click on other people's cows. With every click on your cow, you earn a point, so one day you can trade points for a nicer cow. "How much pot does one have to smoke to play this?" you might say. I do not have any data to back that up. Yet this game, which was meant as an illustration of the stupidity of online games, was a hit.

Next time you are offered a badge for doing something several times, think whether you would actually really want to do it even once.

One key element in games is winning. Jack Welch once said, "I think winning is great, not good — great. [...] Winning lifts everyone it touches; it just makes the world a better place."[7] This somewhat idealistic view is also our vice. We love winning so much that we go to incredible lengths to achieve it. Sometimes we go too far — to the benefit of others.

eBay and other auction houses make multibillion-dollar businesses out of our desire to win. We enjoy the tension, we bid, and we win. In the end, we often overpay and suffer of what is called the winner's curse of auctions. In fact, auctions are the proven perfect means to extract the maximum out of the buyer and reach the highest possible sales price for the vendor. Your only chance for a good deal at an auction is when you are the only one bidding or when you are colluding with other bidders.

Another big business are Groupon-type models. Isn't it a nice game to wait and see if there are enough others to buy the crazy coupon? Actually, it sounds quite lame. I interviewed a bunch of people in Berlin last year outside a Turkish restaurant that had offered those types of group coupons. In this nonrepresentative survey, most answered that they had had a cheap lunch but that they never really wanted to go eat there and that they probably will not come again. I doubt that the restaurant had lasting benefits from this particular promotion.

I had discussed lotteries and gambling above. Their attractiveness comes in part out of this too. Have you heard of beginner's luck? It is an intriguing myth. Take another look. Beginner's luck happens when someone first plays and wins. Then as she likes it, she continues and starts losing as statistics would predict. Of course

---

[7] Jack Welch (2005).

she remembers herself winning in the beginning, and she lives to tell about her beginner's luck. But she is tempted to keep playing because confirmation bias kicks in. The subconscious goes, "I won before, I am good at this, I can prove it and win again." The other people talking about beginner's luck when newbies are at the table further reinforce the idea.

The less-fortunate player loses right off the bat in her first game. In that case, it is more likely that she stops gambling and thus never talks about beginner's luck. She has just always been unlucky.

So do not be fooled. This is not to say we should not play games. After all, humans love playing and we need to play. However, you will want to be aware of what and why you are playing.

Touches and Gestures

Kids' play involves a lot of touching. We hug our loved ones. We pat our friends' back when they are successful. Touch is a symbol of compassion. It makes us feel better and produces oxytocin. The above-mentioned trust hormone is already released at slight touches. This knowledge is no secret.

Waiters that gently brush your arm get more tip. And other deals you are involved in might get slightly skewed against you by the power of touch. I was once working with a real estate agent, and during our conversation she kept reaching out to my forearm. If well played, it is hard to notice.

So raise your awareness. Prime yourself and selective perception will help you notice who brushes you ever so slightly. If you think about the physical interactions before closing a deal, you might be able to consciously account for and thereby negate the effect.

Let us turn the table. Why not use this to your advantage? Ever considered touching the car salesman to make him feel better with you? I am sure you can get a better deal with some practice.

This topic could easily fills a book for itself. If you want to stick around to learn more about gestures and facial expressions, may I suggest *The Definitive Book of Body Language* by Barbara and Allan Pease, as well as *Born to Be Good* by Dacher Keltner of UC Berkeley.

Sexual Heat

You are entering the place; it is kind of dark, your eyes take their time getting used to it. A cute girl with huge fake boobs serves you a beer, and you start chatting about your project to your associate. All the time your mind wanders because not only do those girls look really good — they also put on a distracting show to make sure you look . . . and tip.

The late J.R. Ewing in *Dallas*, the 1978 TV series, always conducted business in a titty bar. Do you think that was wise? Apparently for him it was because the series was one of the most successful ones in TV history. But the story above was not J.R.'s of 1978 *Dallas*. It was mine in Houston more than 30 years later. Imagine doing business in the oil industry and finding yourself talking about large deals over a beer and a few girls dancing around you. Grossing you out? Initially, this was a little unsettling to me as on top of the attraction came the somewhat unfamiliar environment. But ultimately, I took it as the practical experiment I needed to write this section.

While arousal is a pleasant feeling, it does not necessarily yield pleasant outcomes. Sexual arousal short-circuits our mind, and we act totally nuts by our own standards. Would you have unprotected sex with a stranger? Only 12% of participants could see themselves doing so. However, once aroused, 31% went for it. That is almost a threefold increase. And there are much nastier things we are apparently willing to do when aroused. Studies show that we grossly fail to predict the effects of sexual arousal on our decisions. The above was only a moderate example.

Here is my clear-cut advice. Only make purchases or decisions while absolutely calm and nonaroused. If you plan to spend money in an environment that sexually arouses you—hey, J.R.—plan ahead how much to spend, leave your credit card at home, and bring only the cash you want to spend. I am convinced that J.R. was only such a fearsome businessman because he knew not to look at the girls.

Not looking is actually the only way. Our ability to understand and control ourselves does not increase with experience.

Do you want to try it for yourself? Go to hotornot.com and start rating the other sex. Even though you have read this, I bet you cannot stop until a string of some really ugly pictures appears.

For men, this is especially tricky. It is not just an urban myth that they are in general much hornier. When they are primed with opportunities to mate, loss aversion is not only nulled but even inverted into a risk-seeking behavior. Men try to show off what great guys they are. This can be as simple as seeing pictures of attractive women, and men are suddenly more inclined to make status-enhancing purchases. Women, instead, even become somewhat more loss-averse and caring.

Women are more susceptible to men who have high testosterone and higher spending habits during ovulation. Also, women tend to sexy up their wardrobe during that period when they are under the impression of competition from other attractive women. This effect is limited to appearance-enhancing items, e.g., jewelry and clothes. Next time, when it is your time, think twice if that supermodel on the cover of your favorite magazine is really a credible competition before you go out to upgrade your outfit.

Truth be told, sexual arousal pulls a big readership. Yet this works for any type of emotional arousal. So do not shop for weapons while you are mad at someone — you will only spend way too much, even if you do not intend to really harm the person. (Legal disclaimer: Do not harm anyone!) Do not go shopping for food while you are hungry. You will not only like everything but also your decision making will be clouded. Any form of real temptation leads to some sort of arousal. That is why stepping back and calming down is so important and so difficult — because marketers specifically try to keep you aroused.

Resist Temptation

"'I do not want to live the life of a Boxster,' Dan Ariely told the *New York Times*, 'because when you get a Boxster you wish you had a 911, and you know what people who have 911s wish they had? They wish they had a Ferrari.' [...] he started by selling his Porsche

Boxster and buying a Toyota Prius in its place. [...] That is the lesson we can all learn: the more we have, the more we want. And the only cure is to break the cycle."[8]

Guess what, even if you have never driven a 911, you might actually remember it. Crazy? A study in the *Journal of Consumer Research* has shown that advertising can implant false memories. And I distinctly remember driving a Porsche 911 Turbo even though I never did. The research shows that as we recall our memories, we rewrite them as well. However, the farther away the original incident and the more recalls influenced by how we actually wanted the experience to have been like, the more our memory changes. Until we "know" and believe. In the experiment, students were shown a vivid advertising of an imaginary popcorn brand. Afterward only part of the group was given a sample, and the rest (the control group) got another task. After a week, when questioned, members of both groups were equally likely to claim that they had sampled the product itself and to describe its taste. False memory implemented in one session.

It is called the "false experience effect." Scary. Well, my Porsche experience took years to grow, and today I am even more sure it happened than events that have certainly happened. This effect of creating false memories — that can be even stronger than real ones — is commonly accepted in science but poses immense legal and moral challenges.

Watch out for ads that create or build on fake memories. As *Wired* magazine writer Jonah Lehrer

---

[8] Ariely, Dan (2008).

admits, he distinctly remembers drinking Coke out of glass bottles in stadiums when he was younger. Every Coke ad he sees builds on this happy feeling. A feeling that cannot be true as glass bottles have been prohibited for security reasons for ages.

With this knowledge, you could even skip the fun altogether and just build the memory yourself. You are in doubt? Well, why do elder people always tell us how great everything used to be? Every time they tell us, they reinforce their "memory."

To sum up, shield yourself and know how easily you can be manipulated. Be aware. Heighten your defenses against what you see. Dissect your perception. Why do certain things appear that way? A little paranoia will do no harm. And to be on the safe side, try the exercise in the box below.

Becoming Aware of Your Awareness

Strong feelings tend to go directly to our subconscious. Therefore, resisting takes some practice. Here is a little trick my psychologist friend Aaron Shepherd has taught me.

He asks his clients to go through a two-step process. You can do this right now.

First, start to be aware of whatever you are doing. Whether that is reading this book, pouring yourself a glass of water, or tensing up after someone slighted you. Don't judge; just be aware.

Then raise your awareness to the awareness of what you are doing. Thus in this case, you will be aware that you are aware of your current reading.

In the beginning, this feels a bit strange especially as you will find it hard to concentrate on your base activity during this exercise. As I can tell from my own experience, with time you will get better. Therefore, he suggests to practice this for one minute every full hour for a while. Put a reminder into your phone. Then, once comfortable, you can invoke the newly found state of mind as you need it.

It will considerably help you regain your composure whether in a moment of attraction or even more severe emotional distress.

Key Points to Remember

- Many things beyond the product or service itself influence our purchasing decisions, such as the setting, advertisement, and salespeople.
- This influencing happens on many levels addressing various motives deeply rooted within our psyche:

  - The *caveman principle* postulates that our desires are largely defined by our history, roaming the savannah of sub-Saharan Africa being hunters and gatherers.

  - The *image effect* describes our urge to represent certain things and to be perceived in a certain way by our peers. Ever wondered what image you would like to portray?

  - Loyalty makes us want stability in our relationships, whether business or personal. Ask yourself whether the other party is just as loyal as you are and if you are consuming too much out of loyalty, which makes you face decreasing returns for each unit consumed.

  - Our own moods impact our purchasing desires and decisions. Awareness of your current state of mind while making a decision can greatly improve your outcome. By now you should know your tendencies and have created your personal cheat sheet.

  - They also call upon our values. So check if that salesperson is just mirroring any value you exhibit. See if you like that product only because the branding appeals to your value set.

- Visual attraction in the form of shapes, colors, and images and TV does things with us beyond imagination. When you see something beautiful, think functionality.

- On a verbal level, we get subtle cues in forms of simple words, paraphrasing, mail, and forms.

• There are also some particular hot buttons:

  - *Prominent features* overshine important facts. Next time something looks overly important, force yourself to additionally consider the less obvious aspects.

  - We can be primed to something and from thereon perceive everything in comparison to that point. *Priming* sets the filter for *selective perception*.

  - *Herding*: Refers to the behavior of doing too what other people are doing already. In an extreme scenario, you can be in a herd with yourself. Following is not decision making.

  - *Gamification* means setting up things as a game, thereby enticing us to play. Playing then comes at a cost of time and money, and even winning can hold the winner's curse.

  - More or less obvious touches make us willing to pay more, so watch out for them.

  - Sexual tension short-circuits our decision-making processes. We do what we usually would not do. Therefore, protect yourself in advance if you know you might be exposed to anything of sexual attraction.

  - The *false experience effect* makes us remember

events that have never occurred. Brainwashing and total recall are not that far off!

- Try to resist immediate temptation and evaluate why you are tempted before you give in. Then enjoy!

PRICES AND PRIZES

In this part ...

You meet the mother of all parts in this book: Intense, but I think you will see it is what it takes. Here you explore the magic of price tags as well as the occasional lack thereof. This is a carefully curated compendium of the most vicious pricing strategies we face every day. We will talk about trojan horses, charm prices and how gold flakes on food can make all the difference. Time to strike back. Explode the myths of pricing power.

Pricing Rationales

"The price of anything is the amount of life you exchange for it."
— Henry David Thoreau
19th-century American author

"The single most important decision in evaluating a business is pricing power."
— Warren Buffet
American business magnate

In the classical economic theory, the markets serve to find the ideal price. A fair price that allows for the producer to sell all his goods and the consumer to buy as much as he needs. The price drives demand and supply to a matching point where both parties share the benefits of the sold good. This model, however, relies on a number of assumptions that are hardly ever true in reality. You will see in this chapter that the fair price provided by classical economic theory is an illusion in more cases than most of us assume. Producers have a huge interest and leeway in setting prices. In naming prices, they communicate with the consumers. But what message do buyers understand consciously and subconsciously? Let us look at some principles of setting prices and the tricks employed to shift value toward the sellers.

The following four principles are a brief intro to help you understand the vendor as well as your appropriate defense strategies. Sometimes you might find them referenced in pricing negotiations. While these models are described in succession, in practice they will often be combined.

Cost-Plus Price

The price is set by adding a markup to the original acquisition or production cost of the item. In this case, fair means a fair margin that allows the producer to survive and earn a nonobscene profit. Generally, that is a good starting point for consumers. To improve your outcome in a negotiation, you can address the cost and/or the margin.

For example, in the case of work done at your house, you can help looking for cheaper material suppliers. The construction firm you deal with is an agent and does not care too much about your savings on the material. Or you might discuss their margin, which will be hidden in the contracting fees.

Whatever you buy, you will want to make sure the vendor is not falling victim to the *ownership bias* described in the beginning of this book. Imagine you are trying to sell something. As you contemplate doing that, you will be replaying all the memories you have had with that item, whether it's your old tennis racket, your camera, or some old CDs. In a way, they are all emotional luggage. And that does not get lost easily. Thus anything you buy, used or pre-owned, is almost guaranteed to have an inflated price tag. Do some research and make an adequate offer. If the seller does not approach a reasonable price point, leave it. Sometimes you can influence by helping reduce the perceived value. But be careful about invalidating childhood memories and such as it is really hard for anyone to understand that other people do not share their feelings.

When addressing cost, two categories are important: fix and variable ones. Say you are commissioning someone to put new drywall into your home. The contractor will use tools and drywall. He needed to buy those tools at some point in time and amortize them over a longer period, doing work for you and others. These tools are part of his fix cost. They will always be there, no matter what—even if he doesn't use those particular ones on your site. The drywall is only purchased for your project, and the smaller or larger your project, the less or more drywall will be required. This is his variable cost. Other fix costs are, for instance, salaries for his employees or rent for his office. Variable costs also include the wallpaper and paint.

You will want to discuss the major cost items individually to bring them down. The next step would be to aim for a negative margin. This means that the seller will not be able to recoup all of his fix cost. It sounds harsh, but a deal like this might still be worthwhile if the seller does not have better alternatives.

However, as you negotiate, a clever seller will never go below his variable cost unless he sees no other way to sell the merchandise and keeping the merchandise would result in greater loss. This can be the case for perishables such as fruit on a market, a newspaper at night, event tickets, or an end-of-season fashion clearance.

How far you will want to go also depends on whether it is a one-time spot sale or an ongoing relationship with many more interactions to follow. In any case, researching the variable cost will significantly help your cause.

Competitive Price

This price is based on the other players in the market. It works the better the more similar and comparable the merchandise is. Bananas from Dole and Chiquita can be expected to cost about the same. Typically, a price determined this way will be higher than the cost and a minimum markup. Otherwise, the vendor will choose not to engage in this type of business in the long run. There is no general rule whether a competitive price is higher or lower than a vendor-imposed cost plus price. The competitive price is the price determined by the idealistic classical economic scenario always assuming perfect, i.e., maximum, competition. This is the fairest price for both vendor and buyer. Yet there are two seller strategies to get around this: collusion and differentiation

In markets with commodities — i.e., easily comparable goods such gas and bananas — we oftentimes find only very few suppliers, which reduces competition. Additionally, they tend to collude — either openly, in a hidden way, or in an indirect manner as collusion is illegal in many parts of the world. One of the results of collusion is prices inflated to take more money off the table than necessary.

There is not much a consumer can do in this case except acknowledge the standardized characteristics of the goods and find no-name players or new market entrants. Does your car really need branded gasoline? There are national standards as to the octane rating, and that is all you need to know. Even a luxury sports car does not need fully synthetic gas with an octane rating higher than the manufacturer's recommendation as it cannot make use of it.

When competition gets more intense due to more players in the market, typically, the producer will try to differentiate his goods. The goal is to make you believe you cannot find them anywhere else. Indeed, a Chrysler is different from a Ford. But is it really a meaningful difference, on a functional level? Both vehicles get you from A to B and are pretty reliable. We will discuss differentiation in detail in a later chapter.

No Discount Policy

Have you ever shopped a store with a low-price guarantee? Chances are you have and like most of us have not asked for a discount because they already have a low-price guarantee. But what does that really mean? A low-price guarantee is actually a signal to all the other shops out there, indicating that it is not worth undercutting this store as it will simply match the best offer. Using some game theory, you can easily prove that this leads to prices higher than the competitive price. This policy effectively cripples competition, and the best strategy that follows for stores is to set a high price and compete on other features. For you, this low-price guarantee should be a definite indicator to ask for a discount (which will be hard — but possible), or go to another store.

As a buyer, you should always openly compare the merchandise to competing products whether you would actually consider the other ones or not. There are many publicly available credible sources for test results. Those can provide you with some good ammo.

Another means to counter your dealer is to invoke the share of wallet illusion. This means alluding to the fact that you have to distribute your funds across many different expenditures. Thus there is competition not only within but also among expenditure categories. Make it clear that while the Cadillac is the car of your choice, you will also have to go on a vacation on Fiji to make your wife happy. Too bad you can only spend the money once. Suddenly, as the unique merchandise competes with many other things, it gets cheaper.

Value Price

The value price is based on how useful something is to the buyer, i.e., how much utility it provides. In this sense, fair is what provides a value in excess of the price to the buyer. This will most likely be the most unfavorable proposition to you so far as the vendor will strive to leave you only with a minimal benefit, retaining most of the value to himself.

One of the most prominent examples for this pricing strategy is software. Software vendors often make assumptions about the utility generated by their offering and then price their product accordingly.

During sales conversations of corporate software this might even be openly discussed and used as an argument to justify the price.

So it seems like a fair deal, where you make the most of your money. But is it really the best deal for you?

How to counter value price offers? Always be weary when you see one. Carefully consider what the true value is by using your one-hour rule. If possible, play it down. Does the merchant know the utility you derive from something? Software you buy online does not differentiate among customer groups. They are simply targeting anyone who feels his time is worth enough to make the offer worthwhile.

If there is a salesperson involved, he will try to find out how much value you derive and try to find a solution that is affordable to you and at the same time as highly priced as possible. So never tell an antiques dealer how much you love that chest or how rare the craftwork is. Always pretend to just accept it "as is." Buying must sound like a burden that the seller has to ease on you.

However, against all stonewalling, vendors have a secret weapon. Auctions are a great way for a vendor to determine your honestly expected utility. During an auction, we reveal it by making our offer and increasing the bid at least as long as we still see a benefit larger than the price. For us, an auction combines three issues, none of which we aspire:

1.   Instead of negotiating a price down, you are negotiating a price up—at least for most standard auctions.

2. Instead of the seller competing with multiple other vendors for your money, you are competing with other buyers for the item.
3. We take partial emotional ownership as soon as we enter the auction and thus cannot get out of it. This ownership bias skews the odds in the favor of the seller. In the end, we are hit with the so-called winner's curse, having unwittingly bought an item for a price possibly even exceeding our utility.

Your takeaway: Auctions are the most dangerous form of a market to participate in — if you are the bidder, that is. If you still decide to participate, write down the highest amount you are willing to pay before starting the bidding. Then do not go over the amount! Otherwise, your ownership bias delivers the winner's curse on you.

Arbitrary Price

In some cases, prices are set to totally arbitrary figures. How much should a star be worth? (Yes, you can buy celestial body for as little as □20 at http://www.universal-star-registry.com.) How much should one pay for a new economy stock? The answer to this questions heavily depends on the state of the bubble. Suddenly, fair is whatever price is named.

This works because we do not know the true value of things. In some cases, the price is actually an indication or even a determinant of the value. Neither do we know the true cost or the true utility to us. This also works to a certain degree for goods where we have a good idea of a reasonable price range. If you are to estimate the price of a DVD rental, any guess from $0.50 to $5 would be valid. Even beyond that. Why should it cost what it costs?

You think this is far-fetched? Well, when was the last time you sent a text? I hope you cannot remember.

Much to my surprise, my friend Lindsay told me that she had cancelled her texting plan and even had her carrier disable the texting feature entirely after some discussions. I didn't even know this was possible. Looking into this, I found that ATT charges $0.20 for a text message if you do not have a $20/month plan with unlimited texting. So if you don't, that translates to $1,497.97 per megabyte. Considering that you can also get two gigabytes for $20 a month, this is a pretty hefty fee. But that is how much we like texting and how much telecom monopolies are able to extract from our pockets. It makes the $20 plan look like a steal, but using WhatsApp or TextNow, you can do it for *free*. With all we said above, this should be enough for you to cancel your texting service and promote those two apps to your friends.

Paying the Price of Fairness

The "willingness to pay must be exploited to the full," says the founder and chairman of Simon-Kucher & Partners. It is an acceptable and expectable goal for a profit-maximizing company. Yet consumers are not profit maximizers. We settle for what we think is fair, not for as much as we can get. We are fair and generous at heart and thus do not take everything that is available for free and even behave altruistically in many instances.

Therefore, in accepting a price, fairness is paramount to us. We do not like to be or rather feel cheated. Yet as we have seen, fairness in pricing can have many meanings:

- Fair is whatever the cost of the item plus a modest margin (or in some cases even a markdown).
- Fair is whatever the market price is.
- Fair is what provides a value in excess of the price.
- Fair is whatever price is named.

Consequently, businesses strive to shift us in their favor on the above fairness ladder, often mixing various pricing rationales. They can take the lion's share and we still feel fairly treated. Everybody is happy, except — without noticing — you do not have any money in your bank account to pay for your kids' college tuition.

Hardly any well-versed seller will use a cost plus price on his own accord as it is "too" fair. It merely sets the bottom range of how far she will go. If, however, you are on a cost-plus-price line of thought, you will hear arguments about value and utility driving you away from the margin idea toward the value price. If you are in a competitive price mind-set, positive differentiation can be used to increase the economic value to you and thus shift from a competitive price to a value price. In plain English, by making ordinary things seem extraordinary, they can fetch a higher price. More tricks below — especially on how to get to the arbitrary price.

Our irrationalities greatly help in making us overpay, while we still maintain our unwavering and ignorant belief in fairness. Let us delve a bit deeper into those irrationalities.

The Pity Premium

Sometimes fairness seems to have a particular irrational twist. A study looked at a producer, committed to using cost plus pricing, who experienced a 13.3% drop in the cost of his raw materials. It was found that he does not have to drop his price. We still perceive it fair, even though we know how he prices and how his costs dropped. I call this the pity premium because if you act accordingly, you only pay out of pity to the producer — and everyone else will pity you.

How do we decide on accepting an offer? Our hate of unfairness is so big that we battle for fairness even at a cost to ourselves. A famous experiment, the ultimatum game, shows that we would rather punish all the players, including ourselves, than allow the others to gain something that we cannot have.

This game models a typical sales interaction where you are offered something and can choose to buy. In this game, one of two players is handed $10 and asked to give any portion of that money to the other player. However, the other player then decides whether he accepts. If he does, both players can afterward keep whatever money they have, and they will never meet each other again. If he declines, nobody gets anything. So one could be "fair" and pass on half of it, or be super nice, as the other guy looks a little beaten and offer him $7. Or of course, one could offer only $3 — the "he did not earn it, so why should he get anything?" rationale. Or nothing at all. But of course one has to keep in mind how the other party will perceive the split. Will he reject, making me lose too? Or will he accept? In the experiment, it was found that most people will still accept $3 but reject $2.

Largely the same results apply to somewhat bigger amounts as well. But with extremely high amounts, the proportion kept by the seller increases—i.e., the proportion offered is lower despite the total amount offered being larger. And we tend to expect less of a fraction when the amount is larger. The bigger the cake, the smaller the pie the receiving party is happy with. While this might be clever when actually eating cake, it is a strategy that will make the rich richer and the poor poorer in an economy as a whole. Imagine Richie Rich making millions of dollars a year on his investment income. He pays 14% in taxes. Michael Middleclass earns only $50 thousand a year and pays about 18% income tax. And if Michael gets a raise, he will pay overproportionally more! These are actual rates from the US tax code. Other countries, especially Scandinavia or France, offer tax rates that rapidly increase with growing income.

In another version of the ultimatum game, it has been shown that by offering two options, say $2 and $1, where either one can be chosen or both can be vetoed, chances for a deal increase significantly. The low $1 makes the still-low $2 look more attractive in comparison. Chances are it will be accepted even though it would have been rejected if presented alone. In fact, an experiment showed that people accepted 40% less if it was the better of two options than they would have otherwise settled for.

We also find an interesting twist to our fairness perception in a regular buyer-seller relationship. Here, mystically, both parties appear to believe that the seller has a right to set the price. And of course the seller will name terms to his benefit. Thus a higher price appears justified to both parties, implying that the sellers deserve a higher share. So what is offered is always skewed in the seller's favor, and it is more likely to be accepted. We live in a sellers' world. And businesses know this.

What to do?
1. In most cases vendors set a price and we decide to buy or not to buy. Turn the table and do something unexpected: Use your right to the first offer. Set the anchor in any negotiation by naming a price first. You might have to educate yourself a bit on the merchandise you are buying to come up with a good price, but if you do, the anchor will most likely be more favorable to you than any one set be the seller. So if you hear of someone selling his sailboat, don't ask how much he wants — tell him how much you are willing to pay.
2. If you are on the receiving end, do not play ultimatum — make a counteroffer. If you play by the rules of someone else, it will never be your game. Remember this for anything you buy. You might get startled looks at Walmart, but if you are buying a large item, you can do this successfully.
3. If you play an ultimatum game buying something, a good strategy is to offer two prices. Of course when going into a car dealership, you cannot really do that because the dealer will think, *Who is he to offer $17,000 and $19,000 on a $24,000 car? He needs to make up his mind.* But after checking out the car of

your dreams, you can send a friend in with the low offer for that car. He must then stick to that price and not negotiate. In the remote case that the dealer accepts, you come around the corner for the paperwork. If the dealer declines as expected, you walk by five minutes later and make your $19,000 offer. Or if you are alone, you can bid for two cars. Take a more expensive one and bid even less for it than you wanted to spend for the car you originally wanted. Then go back to your real target and offer your desired price.

4. In the end, it boils down to how much being pushed around we allow for. Setting an example, however, is only relevant if there are further meaningful encounters and you need to worry about a reputation that you are building. So consider if you are better off to take what you can get and leave or if you should invest into your reputation.

A lot has been written on negotiation tactics. You might want to have a look at some books, e.g., *Negotiating Rationally* (1992) by Max Bazerman, Margaret Neale.

How the Certainty Effect Factors into Your Willingness to Pay

When was the last time you were 100% sure? Really ask yourself honestly. It is probably quite rare. Therefore, a 100% sure thing is generally awarded a much higher price than a 99% sure thing. A 50% and a 51% sure thing, however, are typically seen very much alike. Doesn't seem like much of a difference, huh? To understand this in practice, imagine the following situation. Someone is aiming a revolver at your head.

The shooter is offering you to buy one bullet. You can name a price, and it is his decision to accept. How much would you pay in the following three cases:

- All six chambers are loaded.
- Three chambers are loaded.
- Only one chamber is loaded.

Kahnemann and Tversky tell us that we would pretty much give up our entire belongings in the first and last case but only a much smaller amount in the three-chamber case. Why is that? In 1, we would certainly die, so we are happy give up everything just for the chance to live. In 3, we are just as scared, and we can make sure we will live. So we pay for our sure way out. In 2, we might survive anyway, and we are offered to purchase an increase of our chances of survival by only 16%. So it's hardly worth the pain of giving up all we have.

Doing the math, however, in all cases all we can buy is a 16% additional chance of survival, which we value quite differently. Even if we accept that in this somewhat exaggerated and constructed example, survival is paramount, there should not really be any difference in your willingness to pay between 2 and 3. Remember this the next time someone sells you an insurance policy, a flatrate upgrade, a deal where double winning odds are guaranteed, and everything else involving certainties.

More reading about probabilities in *The Drunkard's Walk: How Randomness Rules Our Lives* by Leonard Mlodinow.

Key Points to Remember

- There are four rationales how prices are set, with the last two usually being the most expensive for you:

  - The *cost plus price* is determined by the cost of supplying plus a markup for the supplier's profit. Working with the seller on his cost is most likely your best bet.

  - The *competitive price* is found by the market forces supply and demand. Here you will want to introduce as many competitors on the supply side as possible.

  - The *value price* is set based on the expected utility of the consumer. Try not to reveal your true utility or play it down. Rather seek a price based on the above two categories.

  - The *arbitrary price* is randomly set (usually in favor of the vendor). Inform yourself and push for a cost plus or competitive price.

- In our average perception of *fairness*, we feel that we deserve at least 20%–30%, whereas the other party gets the rest. Good news, the others think the same. So use your right to make the first offer. Even if it doesn't feel natural to you in the beginning.

- *Certainty Effect*: We are overproportionally willing to pay for the last bit of certainty. This is why high deductibles are such a good deal.

Relativity and Fix Points

"A cynic is a man who knows the price of everything and the value of nothing."
Oscar Wilde
19th-century Irish writer

"He who is fixed to a star does not change his mind."
— Leonardo da Vinci
Italian Renaissance polymath

While we looked at four ways to argue for a price above, you might have noticed that—except for the arbitrary pricing—none of them had an incontestable starting point. Even the cost plus price starts with a cost, which is itself a price that was externally determined when sourcing the item.

Even though prices serve as a proxy to facilitate trade, they are just a concept, apparently detached from the value. They are in the eye of the beholder. You decide what price is right for you. And quite naturally, sellers' and buyers' interests and opinions diverge.

Coherent Arbitrariness

Imagine something arbitrarily priced. How much to pay for an old Beatles record at a vintage media store? Or the Rolling Stones one? Which one is more valuable? You might agree that the Stones are certainly eight times more valuable than the old and worn childhood book of Tom Sawyer. Some store might price the Stones at $15, another at $50, or even $250 if the condition is like new. If Tom Sawyer is priced accordingly, you will subconsciously perceive it all fair.

As a rule, even though we cannot commit to a specific value, we will be pretty rigid on our relative assessment of those values. This mix of conviction and uncertainty is called coherent arbitrariness.

Where can you use this to your advantage? If you are at a garage sale, remember you are not negotiating the price of one item, but for all the items. So pick one you can negotiate down the easiest to start with. Chances are, the owner will then align other prices accordingly without much ado.

Relativity of Alternatives

Now that we have just bought some vintage records, let us go find a Blu-ray player to illustrate what role relativity plays in determining prices as well as our choices within a product category.

Say you want to buy a new Blu-ray player and do not have a clue how much one would be. (You can try this at home with anything that you do not know much about for the most significant effect.) As of this writing, Google Shopping shows a range of $74 to $234 on the first page for "Blu-ray Player." Which one would you chose? Be honest to yourself. I guess you would probably pick one in the $100–$150 range.

Why do I guess? It is because we instinctively compare. Most people settle for the midpoint, even though some exhibit a different behavior. There are four stereotypes: affluent luxury buyers, frugal spendthrifts or tightwads, average consumers, and random pickers. Which type are you? Despite some influence by our character, the general tendency is to settle for the midpoint. This tendency even remains if the sample is changed to a premium or low-cost one on purpose or without us knowing. Look at this for some more illustration:

A search for "Blu Ray Player Denon" (a higher-profile brand) shows listings for $355 through $1,430. Ouch, that is expensive, but suddenly the $234 player seems like a pretty good deal. After all, you will own the player for a while, so why not? That is why a salesperson in a HiFi store will most certainly invite you to sit in the demo room and listen to the $15K set of speakers even if you only want a small compact stereo.

By the way, looking a little further, I found a nice Samsung for only $63, and I am sure you can even do better. Markets expand further than your eyes can see at first glance, and some research can pay off handsomely.

If you cannot believe this yet, let us look at another experiment. Imagine you see two types of beer on the shelf. A store brand — taste rated 50 out of 100 — sells for $1.80, and another branded one for $2.60, rated 70 out of a 100. Which one would you buy? In an experiment at Duke University, about twice as many students bought the premium beer.

What happened after introducing a third beer at $1.60 rated 40 out of 100? Nobody wanted the new beer. However, the portion of students buying the store-brand beer at $1.80 rose from 33% before to 47%. That is how the supercheap beer actually can help the store drive business to the midprice beer.

A similar effect appeared when instead the store introduced a premium brand at $3.40 rated 75. A total of 10% of the students actually bought the premium beer, but now 90% (up from 66%) bought the brand beer and nobody bought the store-brand beer.

I recently wondered why my supermarket suddenly had two store brands of yoghurt. That's why.

Or consider the full screenshot from the previously referenced e-mail service Sanebox.[9]

Monthly	Yearly	2 Years
Sanity for the price of a latte	Movie tickets for the family can cost more	Dinner for 2 can cost more
$4.95 /month	**$55** /1 year	**$100** /2 years

Source: http://www.sanebox.com

What would you chose? After doing some math, you will see that the savings for the yearly offer are a meager $4.40 over the monthly one. If you ever decide

---

[9] http://www.sanebox.com/pricing retrieved May 19, 2012.

to cancel this service, waiting for the end of the term will most certainly eat up all those savings. And in a time where about half the couples get a divorce, an e-mail service is *not* for life.

Introducing a third alternative that few or nobody really wants can drive demand toward a specific alternative that a shop wants to move. In general, we can always see a *reversion to the middle* if there are multiple options. The effect that comes into play here is *extremeness aversion*. Extended surveys of daily shopping items have shown that, in case of uncertainty about a fair price, we tend to avoid the extremely cheap or extremely expensive alternatives. We shy away from the best or worst quality, from the smallest or largest variant. Feels odd once you know how this middle can be influenced, doesn't it? So next time you see three options, think twice before settling for the middle. It most likely has the highest margin for the store, but how well does it really fit you?

Pricing is relative, and you have to choose what to compare. If you are looking for something cheap that day, resist looking at anything expensive in the same store. Selecting the comparison group is as important as choosing the eventual item for purchase.

Contrast Effect

In another case, a clever HiFi salesperson might lure you into his store with a $150 Blu-ray player that, upon inspection, looks really crappy — already from the outside. Then you will be shown a $170 player that looks terrific. Are you going to ask if there is a cheaper one? Probably not. The $150 *decoy* completely blinded you. Even if you see the $63 player in the showroom, you will most likely assume that it does not have the picture quality or another key feature that the $170 player has, and you will gladly believe without even asking.

Let us expand on this with a further experiment: MIT students are said to be pretty intelligent. So look at the experiment that was conducted among MIT's Sloan MBA students with the real-world offer of the *Economist* magazine. They could select any of the following subscription options:

- online-only for $59
- print and web for $125
- print-only for 125$

As one would expect, nobody picked the print-only option. Puh! A total of 16% picked online-only and 84% picked the combo. At the same time in the next classroom, participants were given the choice without the print-only option. Should it matter? It does — a great deal. Here, 68% picked the online-only subscription and 32% the combo. Introducing the decoy (print-only) made the average Sloan MBA student spend $34.32 more than he would otherwise have. Do not worry — at Berkeley they would not have fared any better.

"How is this possible?" You might wonder. We understand that the offers print versus online are not easy to compare, so we put a lot of conscious effort into our decision. But it's easy to compare print including online versus print-only — especially if they come blatantly at the same price. So our brain once more goes haywire, and we pick the combo, forgetting about the cheaper option altogether. This is an example of the *contrast effect* induced by the decoy. We prefer an item that is clearly better than another, ignoring how it compares to all the other possible options.

This comes into play in many scenarios of complex purchases. Imagine buying a new laptop. There are so many variants. Instead of comparing them all, you might just pick one that is significantly and evidently superior to one other model. A clever salesperson will show you just those.

Side Note about TV Quality

Could you really see enough of the difference between the premium TV and the middle-class TV? Actually, a TV set's performance is usually not the limit, but the media. So in the store you see the most brilliant media that drives the sets to the max (and you will find TV sets that they do not want to sell as much, less carefully adjusted.) At home, with your highly compressed cable TV and DVDs whose quality is often limited by the recording of the original motion pictures, the inferior set can be as brilliant as it ever gets — for your eyes and your purse.

Anchoring

Anchoring means fixating our mind on something, especially a number. It happens by merely thinking about one. Once the anchor is set, your mind builds pricing expectations relative to that number for whatever you are purchasing right now. This works whether the number given is reasonable or far from it! For evidence, look at experiments where people were asked to note the last digits of their social security number (which are completely random) on a sheet of paper and then requested to bid for a random product. In that case, we see that higher social security numbers mean proportionally higher bids.

It is still being discussed how carefully one has to think about a number for the subconscious to acknowledge it as anchor. However, indications are that anchors are set fairly fast, as the above-mentioned example illustrates.

We meet a variety of anchors in real life. Walk along Chicago's Michigan Avenue and the surrounding streets. You can find a $14,000 Ralph Lauren handbag in the window. Or if you are interested in watches, you might have heard of the Hublot "$5 million," the latest model that was introduced into the market at a price tag of $4.75 million. Not only is the watch covered in diamonds to the extent of hiding any visible metal—18K white gold by the way—but also its name calls out how expensive it is. Hardly anyone in his right mind would buy this watch, or the Ralph Lauren bag. But if an amazing watch or bag costs this much, how much then is fair for an everyday bag or watch? Or for something else in the store, like a sweater, a belt, or a keychain? Probably much more than you would have otherwise considered.

The $5 million watch might never be sold, or only a few times, same with the $14,000 handbag; but the keychains, belts, and other accessories account for a substantial portion of those companies' sales. Voila, the anchor at work. That is why everything on Michigan Avenue is more expensive than anywhere else in the city. When you buy a "regular" $2,500 purse, your subconscious will think, *Wow, I saved over $10K.* That is the idea. As publicist William Poundstone pointedly wrote, "items that don't sell can change what does."

Next time you see someone wearing a pair of Chanel sunglasses, remember they are basically a sign screaming, *I have volunteered to be mugged for the better part of the price tag. But hey, they are beautiful!*

This is not limited to luxury items: "These effects of context on choice can naturally be used in sales tactics. For example, Williams- Sonoma, a mail-order business located in San Francisco, used to offer a bread-baking appliance priced at $279. They later added a second bread-baking appliance, similar to the first but somewhat larger, and priced at $429—more than 50% higher than the original appliance. Not surprisingly, Williams- Sonoma did not sell many units of the new item. However, the sales of the less expensive appliance almost doubled."[10]

The same happened when we introduced a premium maintenance package at one of my previous jobs. We should not have been surprised to see sales of our regular package take off, while the premium one did not sell at all. These types of anchors make consumers reframe their decision from "Do I need this?" to "Which one do I need?" So remember, not buying is always an option too.

If you feel that luxury is not your world, join me in looking at the most basic human need: hunger. Whether at an Applebee's, Red Lobster, or a gourmet temple, in the way described above, high-priced entrees act as anchor and raise the revenues for the restaurant, even if nobody buys them. As a matter of fact, people often buy the second most expensive dish

---

[10] Shafir, Eldar, Itamar Simonson, and Amos Tversky (1993).

on the menu. Think about this when you enter Daniel Boulud's, a NYC restaurant. He offers a burger for a whopping $150 stuffed with double truffles. Other even pricier ones come with Kobe beef, more truffles, and gold flakes. Nobody in his right mind would ever buy this. What it does, in any case, it makes the $50 steak look like a great deal.

Well, one might say there is still some reason out there—one $175 burger outfit had to file for bankruptcy recently. Maybe enough people caught onto the concept and started out by finding the cheapest item on the menu and working their way up. Anchoring works both ways. It's your call at which end of the table you choose to take a seat.

Aging Anchors

When a sailor sets anchor, it will hold for a long time. Eventually, it will nudge and gradually move. It will never let go entirely unless the chain breaks. Our subconscious anchors behave similarly. An anchor we once set will influence us over a series of decisions and only gradually lose its effect. Over time, it will go away entirely, but significant effects have been shown after a week or even later as we will see.

Imagine moving from LA to Pittsburgh, most likely you will spend the same amount for housing (or only slightly less) and afford a much more luxurious space as the average Pittsburgher on your income level would. On the other hand, you would squeeze yourself into a smaller studio if you moved the other direction. In both ways, your past housing cost serves as an anchor. Recently, I moved from Ann Arbor, Michigan, to Cologne, Germany, and, knowing this, was able to shave a third of my monthly rent without even slightly compromising on my standard of living. Had I just looked for something in my well-acquainted price range, I am sure I wouldn't have had any problems spending more money. But to what benefit?

Such a long-range effect works only for anchors that you have become very accustomed to. No need to worry that test-driving a $100K car once makes you overpay for cars your entire life.

Anchoring Professionals

With all these anchor effects that make us arrive at subpar decisions, by now you probably think that that is why you always knew to rely on expert help. You had an appraiser for the last property you bought, and you have taken a car mechanic friend with you when you got your last pre-owned vehicle. Bad news. Anchors work with professionals too.

Look at the following study about a staged lawsuit: Four groups of mock jurors were asked to award damages in a case where the defendant had been found liable. They were all told that the defense had suggested 50K, but the plaintiff's attorney's suggestions were varied from 100K to 700K for each group of jurors. The outcome ranged from $90,333 to a staggering $421,538. While the jurors always found the plaintiff's demand too high, they nonetheless increased their award almost in a linear way. This effect is even continuous — though in a mitigated manner — when outrageous demands (in the billions) are put forward. A boomerang effect, where they would award lower amounts in response to crazy amounts, cannot be found. Now you might counter that the jurors weren't professionals but ordinary people working in a professional environment.

Therefore, look at this example of true experts. It indicates that experts are only slightly less influenced by anchors than amateurs. The study resulted in the following appraisal estimates for one and the same property presented to four groups of amateur prospect homeowners and real estate experts. The four pairs of groups were each told a different current listing price. In fact, the actual current listing price was $134,900 based on a prior appraisal of $135,000. The figures below show the average appraisals of several subjects for each listing price.

Listing Price	Amateur appraisal	% amateur appraisal varies from listing	Expert appraisal	% expert appraisal varies from listing
119,900	116,833	-2.56%	114,204	-4.75%
129,900	122,220	-5.91%	126,772	-2.41%
139,900	125,536	-10.27%	125,041	-10.62%
149,900	144,454	-3.63%	128,754	-14.11%

Source: Norcraft, G. B., and M. A. Neale (1987), p. 93

While we see that the experts appraised generally lower and were less influenced by the listing price, we note that they are still influenced, which they should not be! Being objective is their whole value proposition. The two big outliers were amateur group 4 and expert group 2. Nobody can tell in advance what an appraisal will be worth. Coincidence one might say, but possibly a costly one for you, if you rely on the expert.

Anchoring Strategies

The bad news is, there is no way around an anchor. Even if you know that an anchor has been placed, you will still be influenced by it. All you can do is use this knowledge in your favor and aggressively set the anchor yourself. If you cannot set the anchor for the other party, then at least firmly set the anchor for yourself by defining your target in advance. That way, your anchor is in your mind before someone else can speak up and set his or her anchor. As soon as someone else sets an anchor, try to brush it away without giving it credibility; or if you cannot do that anymore, start considering the opposite. Find arguments why the anchor is wrong and name them all to mitigate the effect.

Setting an anchor works in many cases even with extreme figures. Remember this when asking for a salary raise, a discount, or just about anything. You will not want to insult the other party to the point of no deal though. So instead of making your outrageous demand, just make the other party think about a number that skews the table in your favor. Asking for 50% raise will be considered outrageous, but naming the sales divided by the number of employees—if that is several times higher than your compensation—will make your boss anchor without being offended. A figure like that is memorable and feels somewhat fair. Good luck taking it from here.

Also, next time before calling an expert, make your own guess first, and then consider the cost of an expert and see if he or she will likely get you to your target price. Paying a little more instead of paying the expert might be a better deal for you.

Key Points to Remember

- Our sense of prices is *coherent* and *arbitrary*. We do not have an innate sense for the right price, but we do have a sense for prices relative to another. Therefore, always start negotiating the easiest item first, and then the others can drop in unison.
- *Reversion to the middle/extremeness aversion*: We usually settle for the midpoint when selecting out of a group. Therefore, the composition of the group deserves a lot of focus.
- Stores work with *decoys*, inferior products at a high price point that are meant to discourage us from going even cheaper. So look cheaper!
- In a confusing sample of offers, the *contrast effect* makes us prefer an item that is clearly better than another, ignoring how it compares to all the other possible options. Structuring the various offers and evaluating them in more detail will help you make a better call.
- Whatever arbitrary number we hear, it sets an *anchor* in our mind and makes us compare prices we are considering with that particular number. Therefore, the anchor can drive prices into any direction. As anchors even work on professionals and have an effect over time, your only working strategy is to make sure your anchor is set before you go shopping. Then once you negotiate, name your price first.

Jan Dominik Gunkel

Differentiation

"America has believed that in differentiation, not in
uniformity, lies the path of progress."
— Louis D. Brandeis
Early 20th-century associate justice of the Supreme Court of the
United States

"Don't forget that it (your product or service) is not
differentiated until the customer understands the difference."
— Tom Peters
American business author

This is a key strategy how products are positioned
in the marketplace. It comprises many substrategies;
therefore you will probably have heard this term
ample of times. Among economists, differentiation is a
term to describe the changes in certain features of a
product, the environment it is being sold in, and the
way it is being sold, to differ from other competing
products.

One goal is to reduce competitive pressure by
offering a unique product.

Another goal is to allow reaping as much of the
market as possible by selling the same product with
slight adjustments to various customer groups. As each
prospective customer derives a somewhat different
value from the same product, he also exhibits a specific

willingness to pay. Being able to sell virtually identical products at different price points — that are as close as possible to the maximum willingness to pay for the respective customers — greatly increases the sellers' profits.

From a behavioral point of view, the goal can be formulated as to make us buy that particular product and not all the other options out there in the marketplace. The various forms of differentiation outlined below are found in a combined manner most of the time.

Branding

May I offer you some "hand-cut aged prime rib slow-roasted in rock salt and served au jus and freshly grated horseradish" or a "slice of rib roast in its own sauce with salty horseradish"? Which one tastes better? Surprise, it is the same dish! And there are much more extreme examples. Remember last time, when you did not even understand the description of your food? Nice-sounding menu items conceal simple dishes and fetch higher prices — in part by appealing to a more affluent consumer group.

Moreover, consider the artful presentation of the dish on the plate. All this raises your expectation and willingness to pay. The good news is it also ultimately increases your experience due to the *expectation bias* as introduced before. So you can at least feel good for overpaying for a simple dish. Next time, why don't you take something simple and build the positive expectations regardless of the menu description? If it is a decent restaurant, they literally can't afford to present you with a truly bad dish anyway.

When was the last time you were at Starbucks? Have you ever wondered why you are paying $5.19 plus tax for a cup of coffee? Of course you haven't even done that. But what about a Venti Caramel Macchiato?

The only thing our grandparents would have understood here is that there is something with sweet caramel being discussed. This is product differentiation if not even product camouflage at play. What you are getting is a triple shot of espresso coffee with steamed milk and caramel syrup. If that is what the menu would say, you would hardly pay $2.50, let alone $5.19. It just wouldn't sound right as you know how much coffee costs elsewhere and how much the ingredients are priced. Some might not even buy it at all because a triple espresso is kind of gluttonous, while *venti* sounds like freedom, like sailing, like power. (*Venti* is actually the Italian word for "20," as the cup holds 20 oz.)

Well, Starbucks managed to get us onto a new echelon of coffee pricing by making sure we do not even slightly compare what the baristas serve up with legacy coffee. It is only about psychological triggers. By differentiating the product so much, Starbucks has effectively created a new product category and set an anchor for pricing in this new category: as high as the sky.

Remember the herding we discussed before? That's another behavioral cause that makes the Starbucks philosophy work.

Many other stores are thankful and now offer similar coffee-based drinks and ever more expensive plain coffee.

The above-mentioned strategy of oil companies to push branded gasoline, such as Shell V-Power or BP Ultimate, relies on the same principles of differentiation. We only want the best for our car, and we certainly do not want to take chances with poor fuel.

Packaging

Now let us look at what you actually get. How much is in a cereal box? What is the weight of a nutrition bar? How much is in a peanut butter jar? Ah, you know it? All right, how much was in there last year? The same? Maybe the box had the same dimensions, but most likely it came with more contents. Skippy Peanut Butter, for instance, has a dimple in the bottom of the jar that used to be flat. Now, with the same price for years, it only contains 16.3 oz. but used to come in an 18 oz. jar. No worries about your kids getting fat—they are not eating more, you are buying less.

Next episode: Wait for them to advertise a free additional 10% in the jar.

To counter this, look at the comparison labels that are mandatory in some countries or just do the math yourself to find out the price per ounce. Once you get used to it, doing the calculations will become pretty easy. Good for the consumer, Holiday Market and Whole Foods have begun to show the price per ounce on their shelves. If you realize a product is cheating you, don't buy it. By proactively deciding and finding the best package for you, you can make a big difference. And remember going for the middle of three options is not always your best option. Going for the largest, however, might also be a bad choice. Manufacturers know that we expect larger quantities to be cheapest per unit so they simply make the jumbo pack more expensive per unit, and most people don't even check.

So you think dimples in peanut butter jars are slick? Have you ever realized that your shampoo can no longer stand bottom up? Well, probably the rounded top looks more fashionable. No way. Soap is cheap. So putting less into the container is not even necessary. Instead, by changing the container in a way that you cannot get all of it out easily, you will buy new shampoo a few days earlier than you used to. Since you cannot have your shampoo stand upside down for the night and wait for the shampoo to slowly make its way to the hole, you just throw the remaining shampoo into the trash with the container. Imagine that out of the same 8 oz. container you used to get 40 servings, now you get 4 less. That is 10% less for you and about 10% increase in revenue for the vendor.

The same idea applies to toothpaste with larger holes, so you put more on your toothbrush. An urban legend says that a toothpaste manufacturer was able to increase sales by 40% with this trick.

Sometime ago, I changed from Fructis shampoo to the cheaper Nivea. After a while, I noticed that I literally found myself shopping for shampoo about twice as often. As a result, I was spending more, not less. My hair hadn't needed more washing though. A closer look revealed that the former was way more viscous and therefore much less poured into my hand during the fraction of a second that I typically squeezed the bottle. Only by making a conscious effort was I finally able to reduce the quantity of shampoo per wash without impairing the result. For me, this has proven too much of a hassle, and I am now back to Fructis.

Next time, behind the shower curtain let's not be fooled. You might really want to start rationing toothpaste and other cosmetics.

All right, what then about the famous detergent concentrate? They say you need only one scoop instead of a cup. So the small package lasts longer than the big one. In that case, it is only fair that it is a little more expensive. We pay for power, not for size. In practice, this is very similar to the shampoo case above. Out of habit, we use considerably more of the concentrate than we would need to. Have you ever thought that a little spoon of detergent just can't be enough for the dirty laundry your kids brought home from football practice? There you go. Statistics show that many of us use twice as much of that concentrate as necessary and deplete the contents of the package much faster than anticipated, turning the bargain into a bane. We thus need not only more detergent but also more water for longer rinsing cycles afterward. Lastly, it is bad for the environment.

On a side note, concentrate might even be cheaper for the producers. The smaller packaging and lower weight reduce shipping and storing costs on the entire supply chain. Manufacturing the smaller units allows them to increase the output in units per facility and thus amortize the factories much faster. In most cases, the change in raw material does not considerably add to the cost. Consequently, the cost goes down and the sales price goes up. A strong recipe for more profit.

All this builds on the fact that we do not change our behavior after migrating to a new product.

Not only physical goods are packaged. Experiences and services are as well. For my recent birthday, I got $260 tickets to a Lady Gaga concert, which I thought was expensive as hell. Apparently, I do not know the first thing about pop venues. A quick check on the Internet revealed that tickets for her shows are sold for up to $1,045 — and you still won't be allowed to touch her. :) But there are also tickets for considerably less than $90. So let us have a look at my $260 ticket.

It buys me a seat on the balcony, a dinner with free drinks, as well as a parking pass. So I will end up taking up 50% more space than a spectator on the floor. The dinner won't be prepared by a three-star chef, so let us assess another $20, including the drinks I consume. The parking pass rings up at another $10. Of course there is a nonquantifiable additional value in a possibly better view one could say, but also you are not where the action is. Finally, this makes a total of $75 in additional value versus a price premium of $170. Happy Lady Gaga nets an additional $95 by offering those premium seats. Otherwise, I would have just received the $90 tickets. Too bad for her she can't offer all tickets at the high price. If she did, substantial groups of her fans could no longer afford coming. Consequently, on average concerts with ticket price differentiation claim 5% more revenue than those with single ticket pricing, and I get to enjoy feeling special. A few words in defense of the artist. Of course she doesn't just pocket those additional revenues. There are many parties involved that all earn their share, and it is even likely that the expensive tickets cross-subsidize some of the cheaper ones. Without some spectators paying $260, Lady Gaga might not be able to have such a fancy stage.

By the way, the same applies to airlines. They almost exclusively make their money with first- and business-class travelers, while the cattle class — airline vulgo for economy — barely breaks even. Airline pricing and possible savings alone could fill an entire book. Maybe my next.

Bundles

McDonald's 101: The value meal is the best deal you can get. Burger, fries, and Coke for a little more than the sandwich and the fries, for instance. Great deal, we have learned it, and we believe. The same applies to a bathroom renovation as I am currently observing. Buying everything individually is outrageously expensive; however, procuring a whole bathroom from a construction company gets you a much better deal. Obviously, they have negotiated special prices with the component suppliers that I can't beat. Also, it is a huge saver of time and transaction costs. But then, they define the options. If I want a toilet seat they do not have, I am basically stuck.

Truth be told, generally, bundles are a good deal most of the time — for both sides. By packaging a few things together, the merchant reduces complexity and sells them in one box and you get all the stuff you want at once for a better price. But the world is not that easy. Bundles have a number of caveats that we tend to overlook:

1. **We buy more than we need.** At our favorite fast-food joint, only the large value meal comes with potato wedges, not the small one. So if we want the wedges, we have to have a large soda as well. Studies show that 26% of people who would have

bought small fries a la carte opted for the larger option that came with the bundle. While the price per fry is certainly lower in the bundle that does not help you if you cannot or do not take them home for later consumption. Buying the bundle means also paying for the full bundle. Or if you shop for a Dell, try configuring it with your minimum required specs and maybe it's cheaper than the predefined bundle you saw before. (Beware of the loss aversion when your minimum configuration does not have some of the features of the bundle inspected before.)

2. **We buy stuff we don't want at all.** A total of 15% of people who would not have bought fries at all with their meal suddenly bought fries because a bundle was offered. Moving to a different industry, have you ever wondered why Microsoft Office comes in such strange packages and you often have to buy some applications that you really never use? Or the one Autodesk or Adobe design application that you really need is bundled with other irrelevant tools in a so-called Creative Suite. Bundling this way helps software vendors push a larger portion of their product range at a generally higher price point than in the case of selling everything individually. (We are talking of profit improvement in the range of 20%–35% with clever bundles.) The mathematics behind this involved conjoint analysis and a lot of sophisticated tools. It's some sort of rocket science. But no one said consumers were easy to fool.

3. **It's simply overpriced.** There is no rule that a bundle has to be sold at a discounted rate over the individual items. As a matter of fact, I have seen bundles priced higher than the individual items. Whether that was some kind of honest mistake or a trick to exploit the common understanding that the package price was a good deal, I cannot say.

In the end, merchants decide to offer bundles because they are a highly profit-maximizing strategy for them. We perceive an increased value with the bundle, so we go for it. Welcome, obesity and gluttony.

Indian versus Japanese Bundles

"It depends" is one of economists' favorite answers. Same with bundles. Apparently, we do not like them all the time. Matthew Amster-Burton, author of the book *Hungry Monkey*, offered an example of an upscale Indian restaurant. There we are offered an Indian entree with all sides and features for $28. He loves the place and is happy to wait for an hour before being seated while being served some free samples. Of course the samples are not really free but paid for with his $28 entree. On the other hand, he knows this Japanese noodle place where he has to pick his bowl of noodles for a price and then pay each of the ingredients separately, varying from a few cents to dollars. He loves it too and both times is convinced of getting a good deal. Totally irrational? Here we are back to expectations. As Kit Yarrow, professor at the Golden Gate University, explained to him, "When things are more expensive, you're already paying the higher price of entry to get in there and everything that comes with it feels like a gift," and "if it is cheaper sorts of products, if you can add in something for a

Unbundling

Unbundling is specifically focusing on individual
items instead of bundles — even if they belong together
or are simply sold together. If bundling is such a smart
strategy, why then do we have to talk about
unbundling? Well, in some cases it is even smarter. Joy
has *decreasing marginal utility*, as the economist would
say. In plain English, we prefer multiple gains over one
larger gain even if they total the same value
mathematically.

That is why infomercials will separately promote
each component individually only to sell it in a bundle
afterward. This way, you are enticed with the
maximum benefits while at the same time you are
tempted with the bundle.

Imagine a tool set. At the end of a session, we
believe that we can buy a 135-tool set for $29, which is
only about 21¢ per tool, and that seems really a good
price. But still we will have to spend $29, and
effectively, we only use three tools out of the set: the
hammer, the screwdriver, and the pliers. Now they
cost about $10 each, and most likely they are crap.
How much quality can you get on a 21¢ tool,
considering that the manufacturer and all the other
parties involved in the sales channel also take their
cut?

[11] Amster-Burton, Matthew (2012).

Likewise, when you give presents, you can increase their value by unbundling. To be more specific, make sure to put them in as many separate boxes as possible for increased value perception. I vividly realized this a few days ago on my mom's birthday. Coincidently, I had packed four individual smaller presents and was actually somewhat anxious as I did not have that one special item. Yet to my surprise, she was totally excited to get so many presents as they kept on coming. And to me it felt like she enjoyed them much more than any one "special" gift I could have possibly delivered.

Location Based

Pricing theory knows the term *expected price* because we take into account the context of our purchase. Where do we buy? What mood are we in, and so on. All these factor into how much we expect to pay and thus will be willing to fork over. This is the expected price. A gallon of milk in the supermarket costs $2, but at a gas station we are happy to spend over $5 or more. Why is that? Initially, we paid for convenience of the longer hours and eventually got used to it. It is now part of our commercial culture. Nowadays, there are enough 24-hour supermarkets, and also during daytime, why still pay a convenience premium for something that is no more convenient than the alternatives? Because out of habit, we think it is fair. So we pay.

The same I found at Plum Market in Ann Arbor. They can charge twice as much as the Kroger's just down the road for the identical branded produce. But Plum Market offers all the exquisite delicious items we expect to pay a high price for. That spills over to apples and mushrooms. Also the beautiful store displays and "green," "organic" signs make us feel we are on a luxury farm, where even pigs are treated as kings. Next time, consciously decide which store to go to.

Of course you will have to keep in mind how much time it will take you to reach the cheaper store, so you might still be better off being exploited on one or a few items. When you crave one of the above-mentioned Venti Caramel Macchiatos, finding a Starbucks at your local strip mall is just not much of an option when you are at the gate at JFK.

Learning from what we said about packaging, even a McDonald's Burger on a nice china with some garnishments will taste like a gourmet dish. Try it and serve your friends with take-out! That is why McDonald's has started completely remodeling its stores to come across a lot more upscale. Suddenly, it is very different from the good old junk burger place. In some areas, McDonald's have transformed into a hub of well-dressed businessmen, mostly salespeople preparing their next calls. Especially in some geographies, they are becoming the new Starbuckses.

Remember that last time you took that special someone out for a candlelight dinner? Chances are you paid, and chances are you remember everything about your sweet love. But what about the check? I know, it's almost a heretical question, yet these are the questions researchers ask.

A study compared the menus of romantic restaurants in NYC to restaurants classified as good places to have business lunches. The dishes served in both groups were rather similar. Yet the price differences were staggering. Candlelight establishments charged 6.9% more for appetizers and a 14.5% romance premium for desserts relative to the main course. Of course this might all be coincidence. But if one does not believe in chance, one could easily assume a conspiracy. People on a date do not want to come around as cheap, nor do they have the time to bother too much about the bill. But why such a different romance premium between appetizers and desserts? My hypothesis is that as we are nearing the end of the dinner, tensions increase due to the uncertainty about the following events. So couples are much more likely to drag it out a bit by ordering dessert, without regard for the price, before moving on to the next base.

Watch for keys that indicate expensive food. If you can identify any of them, see if you can get the same value for less at a different venue.

Time Based

Remember when the original iPhone came out? There was such a hype prior and shortly after the launch that masses of people flocked into the stores to get one, waiting in line and ultimately paying $599 in June of 2007. I still have a vivid memory of waiting for a Christmaslike event for several long weeks. If you were one of us, your guts probably still tighten when I remind you of how its price dropped to $399 in August—a mere two months later. A revolution is high-risk high-reward, one might say. And so was the iPhone. If we wanted to be part of the revolution, we had to pay. Once the revolutionaries, i.e., the early adopters, all had their phones, Apple set out to go after the rest of us: those who still needed a good phone, full-screen iPod, and mobile Internet but weren't quite willing to pay the equivalent of eight pairs of sneakers, 300 gallons of milk, or many hours of work. (Remember your one-hour rule.) Today, I wonder how much worse or better we were or would we have been off by waiting two or three months and saving $200 in the process.

Another product group that highly exploits timing is media. If you want to be in the know and read the book right when it is launched, they make you buy the expensive hardcover edition. If you can wait, there will eventually be a paperback. But waiting here means playing someone else's game. So what would I do? I live close to a public library. There I can get everything I want for free. They will even order books for me. In the last three months, I have read close to a hundred books. (Yes, speed reading works.) The choice of buying versus borrowing was an estimated $1,500 choice. Even if you do not read as many books, saving $1,500 over the course of years is still worth considering.

In an even more severe form, this time based differentiation applies to movies. You can spend $15 at a theater, $10 for a DVD, $5 on iTunes, $1 on a Redbox rental, or watch it for free on TV even later. It mostly depends on how much time you have, although we see some intermingling with location (Blockbuster versus Redbox) and product (DVD versus Blu-ray) differentiation as well as other effects. Yet the general trend is still visible.

In the above time-based product differentiation strategy, items are first very expensive, and then the price gradually drops until every last one of us has bought the product. Then a new one is launched, the cycle starts over. Apple only had one price drop, while many other products, e.g., Sony's PlayStation have their price decline very steadily. Of course this only works if the product is attractive and we — for whatever reason — want to have the product early.

Additionally, there is a product pricing strategy, where a product is priced at a certain level from day one, and that price increases over time. Utilities are a classic example, as they oftentimes offer good deals to new customers and then increase their rates during the second year.

In general, you will want to find out what type of pricing strategy is behind the product you are interested in, while resisting the urge to buy immediately. Waiting could make a big difference for you.

Afraid of Eating Spoiled Food?

Is "best before" the same as "not good after"? This is the most common misunderstood verbiage on food packaging and a very effective form of differentiation. Nobody wants to die of food poisoning, so we seemingly rationally do not buy products close to expiry. That in turn leaves supermarkets an overproportionate quantity of soon-to-expire merchandise. Some supermarkets counter this with markdowns already on the day before expiry. Others wait until the day after. In any case, chances are, the items are still good. So be rational and buy them. Even if on average one out of five yoghurts is spoiled, you probably had a 50% discount and thus paid only 2.5 and still got four good ones, which is a mathematical discount of 37.5% over time.

Although it is not as good as that of dogs, humans have an extraordinary sense of smell. It can serve you well at detecting rotten food. Trust me, if your nose smells anything rotten, you will know without much training. Until recently, this was the only way mankind survived to see the next day.

Individual Customer Based

One of the most irritable schemes of price differentiation I found while purchasing brand furniture in Germany. The merchandise is pretty standardized. A sofa can consist of several modules with upholstery of your choice. As I walked through the showroom glancing at beautiful furniture, I found some promising price tags, or so I thought. Unfortunately, these prices just applied to the specific showroom piece, which was already somewhat tarnished, of the wrong color (who buys mint green leather dining room furniture?), or for whatever reason certain not to fit my needs. It is customary to order the piece you want and have it delivered to your home within a few weeks. That is how business is done.

So I speak to the salesperson. We put together my sofa, pick the leather I like—a type of cream—and then she fetches her price list folder and starts calculating. Whooo! It is like three times the price of the piece I saw in the showroom, which, by the way, has been sold already and is just waiting for pickup. And "special leather and bla ..." So we talk about pricing, and she offers a small discount. As I do not seem to get much further with her, I wrap it up and go to another store the next Saturday about an hour away. (It was an expensive piece, so it was well worth the ride.) Dressed elegantly — I sure wanted them to take me seriously — I walk in, we go through the same exercise, and wow, it is even more expensive.

Interesting as his price book looks just the same. But apparently there are different numbers in it. How can that be an MSRP as both salespeople claimed? Again, I note down all the initial prices, negotiate a bit, and leave. The other offer was still way better. But I am getting curious.

Next store, same procedure, same — but different — price book and best price so far.

What I noticed while looking closely at the previous as well as this price book: They had a little number on top of each page. However, it was different each time. Interestingly enough, after doing the math, the number proved to be the multiplier they put on their base price for quoting. It started to dawn on me. All along the salespeople had been taxing me and estimating my buying power to differentiate their pricing accordingly. Then they picked the appropriate price list and quoted. I ended up with offers where the top one was more than double my eventual purchase price. Margins between 80% and 170% were added. I felt not only hurt by the attempts to exploit me so grossly but also surprised by the stark difference in salespeople judgment of my purchasing power.

A furniture industry expert recommends to negotiate for a 20% discount on the market price, which is the average of at least five stores' prices after initial discounts and rebates. I second that from my experience, in most cases (and in far more than most people believe), a 20% discount is realistic, whether you are shopping for furniture, designer clothing, or services. Even for cars and IT equipment, you can get significant discounts if you do your homework.

Customer Group Based

Not in all business can there be a differentiation on individual customer basis as illustrated above. It is just too costly. Imagine Disneyland. We all have different financial capabilities and willingness to pay, but to date there is no practical and efficient way of determining that. So the second best solution is group-based differentiation.

As it can be said that students and senior citizens usually don't have as much of an income, their willingness to pay can be assumed to be lower than that of regular adults. For Disneyland, where a large chunk of the cost is for providing the infrastructure, it makes good sense to provide those special rates. Every additional student covers her *variable cost* (the cost Disney would not incur if this person would not be present, as explained in more detail in the chapter "Pricing Rationales"). Thereby she makes a contribution to the infrastructure cost, albeit a smaller one than an adult. But any contribution is a good one, unless it takes the place of larger contribution of another potential full-paying guest whose spot is taken by that student (for instance, because the park is sold out and there is a bunch of adults waiting outside).

If discriminating publicly is inappropriate, there are other ways. Supermarkets, for instance, have shoppers of poorer and richer background in the same store by offering coupons. Poor ones will spend the time clipping; the rich do not. Thus they pay more for the same goods in the same store.

The same applies to cell phone carriers that offer better rates if you are a member of a certain automobile club or have a specific credit card. Technically, majority of the population qualify for some sort of discount, but most people simply don't bother.

Multifactor Differentiation

Modern technology makes sophisticated differentiation of individual customers possible in unexpected places. Look at online shopping. Some online shops will quote different prices to shoppers depending on the neighborhood they live in as this reveals a lot about their paycheck. There is not much you can do about this as this decreasingly depends on log-in information but more and more on your IP address. It can be located with enough accuracy even without your consent.

For some less advanced among the advanced websites use a privacy-enabled web browser and also double-check with a faraway friend's address if you are asked for one before a price is shown. The only sure thing you can do to get around it is shopping without being logged into the shop and at the same time using some sort of IP masking service like hidemyass.com. With this level of hassle, countermeasures only make sense for expensive purchases.

Another amazingly differentiated pricing scheme is managed by airlines. Virtually every passenger on a plane pays a different fare. This is based on the time of the booking, individual discounts, frame agreements, return flight dates (if you are not staying at least one Saturday night, it is much more expensive as you are probably a business traveler), and much more. You can hate it, but there is a good percentage of passengers in first class paying less than those in economy.

Key Points to Remember

- *Differentiation* allows to sell the same base product simultaneously at various price points. Offers will differ in branding, packaging, bundling, location, time of purchase, and many more factors. You will always want to seek out the cheapest variant.
- Especially *bundles* are treacherous as they make us buy more than we usually want, sometimes even things we don't want at all, while making us believe we are getting a deal. In fact, we are mostly overpaying. Next time, when offered a bundle, consider what you really want, add up the prices, and see if the bundle is really cheaper.

Trojan Free

"Father, burn it."
— Paris to his father, discussing the wooden horse in the movie
Troy (2004)
"There ain't no such thing as a free lunch."
— Unknown

When was the last time someone offered you something for free? A sample in the supermarket? A free DSL trial period? A free box cutter with the power drill?

In Greek mythology, after a long and wearing battle for the city of Troy, Odysseus ordered a wooden horse to be constructed, which was to be gifted to the Trojans in a gesture of retreat. The horse was built, magnificent, a beautiful creation of Greek esthetics. The citizens of Troy were joyfully celebrating, drinking, and rejoicing their victory. However, the horse housed several warriors that — once the horse had been brought into the city — climbed out at night after the festivities to open the gates. From within, the city's walls were broken; what remains of Troy is but a myth. What a sweet present.

You get the picture. What you first see and act upon might just be a small fraction of what is really going on. So it is with free stuff as we will see.

Subconsciously, once something is free, we crave it. We go to great lengths to attain it. Even if we have absolutely no use for it. We even go so far that we buy other things to get the free stuff or accept being hurt in return. Free is an "emotional hot button—a source of irrational excitement," and it takes you long training and focus to resist.

Here are a couple of examples to show you that once we see "free," we go nuts. In an experiment, subjects were offered to purchase either a $10 Amazon.com gift card for $1 or a $20 gift card for $8. Which one would you have picked, if any? Since Amazon.com gift cards are like cash, most subjects opted to buy one and in particular chose the card worth $20. This experiment essentially allowed participants to create a profit of $12 (or $9) out of thin air. A control group was offered either a $10 gift card for free or a $20 gift card for $7. Which one would you have picked if part of this group? Rationally speaking, you are choosing a profit of $13 over a profit of $10. Without much ado, however, people flocked to the free $10 voucher and forwent the additional $3.

Since this seemed somewhat odd, many other studies were conceived. So here is another experiment conducted by Dan Ariely. He invited students to purchase Hershey's Kisses and Lindt Truffles at his university priced at 1¢ and 15¢, respectively. Both a pretty good deal. The result was 73% chose the premium Lindt, and 27% chose the Kisses. Another time, he changed the pricing by dropping each by 1¢, rendering the Kisses free. Suddenly, 69% went for the free Kisses and only 31% chose the Lindt. One cent really did not make much of a difference to the net worth — even among college students. Yet preferences changed to a degree so significant that it cannot be ignored.

The reasons behind this behavior have not yet been fully uncovered. Some theorists go back to the caveman principle, an evolutionary explanation: When humans were roaming the savannah of Africa ages past, life was scarce; and whenever they found anything special, they took it. Sometimes it might have been a cadaver, or a shaped stone to be used as a tool. Nature provided for free, so we took it. All other options, such as hunting, were considerably more dangerous, and prospects were often poor.

Another theory goes back to our intrinsic loss aversion as discussed above. Free seems to come without a potential for loss at first glance.

Additionally, a lot of these decisions happen in the first instant of us spotting something. (Read Malcolm Gladwell's *Blink* for more about what he calls "thin slicing.") Too bad, we often fail to recognize the hidden cost as we will see in this chapter.

Next time you see something advertised as free, ask yourself, how can something be free? If it is of any value, it has some cost associated with it, and someone will have to bear that. So what could this particular someone's rationale be for providing this for free to you? Might there be a better deal hiding behind the fog of some free items? Face it. If there is one thing to teach your kids to be ready for this century, it's to beware of the free.

Let's now look at several shapes and forms of the "free" in the marketplace and the hidden cost they come with. There are six major types of hidden costs: your time, enabling cost, pain, indebtedness, and loss of privacy. The sixth is that you are simply expected to pay later. What should matter to you is the total cost.

The most commonly underestimated one is time. Therefore, it is the first one I am going to introduce.

Paying with Time

Recently, at the mall in fashionable Buenos Aires Palermo district, there was a chocolate sampling, and hundreds of people were lining up. I specifically remember one aggressively orange-dressed gourmet near the end of that line. You just couldn't miss him. After I was done shopping, he had almost made it to the front of the line. Probably waited for half an hour or so. Just to get a free tasting of 20¢ worth of chocolate. Based on the one-hour rule, you can conclude that he effectively values one hour of his time at 40¢.

There are other less evident yet similar situations: When was the last time you attended a free museum day or night? Remember how crowded everything was? It takes more time than usual and you cannot peacefully admire the art. If your goal is meeting people, it's a different story.

Watching free TV, i.e., ad-financed publicly available unencrypted TV, or YouTube videos that are interrupted by ads, is not free either. Advertisers pay for the content being provided, and you pay with your time.

Remember, just about anything you do is an investment of time — even finding and toying with that new free app on your iPhone. Your one-hour rule can tell you if it's worth it.

Paying for Access

Procuring the free item comes with a cost not only of time but also of money. This so-called enabling cost is the gas to get there, the entrance fee to enter the club, the purchase price of the coupon book. The total of these enabling costs can easily exceed the value of the free item or service at hand. Think free car wash 20 miles away.

"There is no such thing as a free lunch." Even the "Free 72 oz. Steak" at the Big Texan Steak Ranch in Amarillo, Texas, is not free. Once you look at the rules, you will see that you have to pay $72 for the steak up front, and they will be refunded if you finish it. Well, even if you take some home, it is probably a good deal for the quantity, but would you really want to spend $72 for a steak dinner? The prospect of the free steak dinner and the competitive instincts have driven more than 50,000 people to try their luck. About 8,800 have made it. Let's look at this one a little closer. How does the free still work with enforced prepay? you might wonder. My guess would be that you see the free and go for it. The challenge spirit further compels you to try it. Then once the waitress tells you that you have to pay up front, the default is moving along and you would have to make another decision to consciously pull out of the deal, at which time also loss aversion will kick in. So there are at least two behavioral tricks that make you stick with your decision and fork over the fateful $72.

Other free-with-purchase offers are even more explicit. "Buy one, get one free." Yet we still think that we get free stuff. What we really get is two items for the advertised price.

On a winter stroll through Chicago, I saw this kid announcing a sale at a suit retailer. I felt cold, so I went in. (Wait, it gets worse.) Dressed in my jeans and sweater, I had no feeling for a suit that day. They sold a few Hugo Boss, Calvin Klein, and other pricey brand-name suits in odd sizes. Although I did not see anything that was to my particular liking, to kill some time, and stay warm, I put one on, tailored by some unfamiliar Italian-sounding company. (Am I really the author of this book?) The salesgirl immediately told me that with this suit, I would get another one for free. The first one for just $499. Bzzzr, like my brain was short-circuited. Little did I realize or care about the poor fit and the unknown brand. We took some measurements for the sleeves and pant legs. They were happy to mail it to my Michigan home. Once I was at the cashier, I saw the damage, including state and city tax plus shipping. Too late to back out. (Of course I could have, had I been stronger.) No way for me to even ever find the store again and complain, let alone return the merchandise. Every day, when I open my closet, I feel pain looking at those two garments. But they are a reminder of my own irrationalities.

So what happened here? First, the old trick of having a few pieces of high-quality high-price merchandise for anchoring, then using the free argument, and finally me defaulting along the path they had nudged me onto.

Paying with Pain

Have you ever attended a trade show and gathered free pens, giveaways, keychains, notepads, and other free trinkets? Remember how your hand was hurting from carrying the bag, which cut into your palm? It felt like a worthy prey nonetheless. Now open that desk drawer and see how much of that stuff is still in there. Unbothered ever since. But it was free. Do you see the point? You might want to have another look at the chapters on what we really need for a good life.

Paying with Guilt

The Romans had a saying: "Do ut des." It refers to our feeling of indebtedness. When something is giving to us, we feel obliged to give something in return. Whether in the short or long run. It is a natural subconscious character trait.

I benefited from this myself sometime ago when I was heading a nationwide charity effort for lower-class children's art education. Among other things, in major pedestrian precincts we were gifting a rose to passersby and subsequently asking for a donation.

Even free sampling in supermarket creates a sense of indebtedness — especially when there is a human doling out the samples. That is part of the reason we don't find sample dispensers in the cookies section but actual individuals inviting us to try.

The invitation for dinner at you friends is very similar. You will have to invite them back. And there are people who don't go because they don't want or can't invite others in return.

Remember that kid in college who used to copy all the homework assignments? The one who never contributed to the group work but somehow managed to get the best grade? While he got a lot for free, he was also the most unpopular kid, I imagine. Right next to the one who never let anyone copy the math assignments.

If you take something without giving back, or if you take something without giving first, you break an implicit social contract. Some people do not understand this: we call them autistic based on a genetic disorder. The line between not being exploited and egoistically benefiting is a fine one. Turning something seemingly free into something really free by not paying or contributing as implicitly expected afterward will make the other party much less likely to conduct business with you in the future and will make you have fewer friends. You will make the world a worse place. By simply refraining from giving in to temptation, you can show that you are smart, save money, and even make the world more interesting because people will wonder, who is she not to want this or that? But be careful when rejecting offers, even small gifts at trade shows, not to hurt feelings. Appreciate the nice pen and the gesture, and explain why you do not take it.

There are some cases where you can be a bad boy or girl without anybody noticing. The group Radiohead published their album *In Rainbows* on

October 10, 2007, online for download. You were allowed to pay, but you did not have to. You could have free-ridden here without any of your friends knowing. Actually, a ton of people did. But some still paid money. In case you wonder, Radiohead made some money with the album; however, it is hard to say how much they would have made through regular channels. A huge contributing factor for them was that they were the first major band to do so and thus got loads of publicity.

Paying with Privacy

Once I knew a guy who ordered a shampoo online because it came with free tampon samples. Just in case you wonder, he did not even have a girlfriend. Well, too bad the tampon company now has his *information* and they believe he is a she. I am curious what kind of junk mail he receives.

In the summer of 2011, I participated in a drawing for a Cadillac CTS-V at the Houston Galleria Mall because I got a free $10 iTunes voucher. Well, because I know I can't change my behavior, I try to outsmart myself. One way is having a separate junk identity that I can use for things that I actually need to have access to. For other stuff, like supermarket memberships, I just use a totally false identity. You will always want to have a couple of those prepared; otherwise the hurdle of making one up is too high and you will just use your real one.

You might wonder why stores don't do anything about it. Here is my take on it:

- Enough people are still honest.
- The cards don't actually offer a discount. They just allow you to purchase at a regular price. All those people who don't have a card, however, have to pay the previously increased list price.
- Cost of enforcing would be too high in relation to the damage done.

Paying Later

Occasionally, I still see cigarette promotions. *Take a free one and get addicted* seems to be the mantra.

A free phone with a monthly plan oftentimes follows the same rationale. I have recently bought an iPhone 4S and saw two deals from different operators. Free phone with a 24-month plan at €89 a month. Or a 24-month smartphone plan at €39 without a phone. The iPhone retails for €629 in Germany. Everything else was identical. A free phone sounds great—especially compared to a €629 one. Let's do the math here. After two years, I will have paid €2,136 for the free phone, including service. (By the way, the phone would have been SIM-locked, so I would have had a harder time selling it, if I ever wanted to switch.) The €629 phone would have cost me €1,565 (€936 for the two years of service plus the phone). That was €2,136 versus €1,565. I was shocked. Apparently, companies know we act this way and they price to benefit from that. The free offer would cost me €571 more over the course of two years. That is about €24 a month. Guess which one I picked.[12]

---

[12] T-Mobile versus O2 in Germany beginning of 2012.

Another common contributor to get stuck in the dumps is taking out a (car) loan. Go to your local dealer and see if there is an offer for a car financing plan without closing cost, with zero interest or without down payment. All this appeals to the same instincts. Yet any loan needs to be worthwhile to the issuer. Once again, what should matter to you is total cost.

So what is a loan? A loan is someone giving someone else money for a certain period of time. Doing so comes at a risk, in particular the risk that the money will not be returned. This is the classic interest portion. However, a loan has to be sold also—i.e., the car salesman receives a sweet commission. There is administration involved around the loan, like credit checks, sending out statements, and so on. Many lenders will make you pay for these services. Some even pay out only, e.g., 96% of the loan amount, but they expect you to pay back the full 100% plus interest. I have also seen a mortgage bank that sends you a monthly real estate magazine while you are on the mortgage. Guess what—they charged a hefty fee for that. Granted, you could cancel the subscription, but I bet few people even noticed that they were paying for that. My parents did not.

There are a number of loan cost calculators on the Internet. All that I have seen just tell you where you end up after interest payments. That is not doing justice to you. All the fees can easily add up to more than the interest. As you have probably figured by now, I absolutely hate loans. If you must get into these muddy waters, don't go for the free but do the math over and over again.

Evernote, ClearSlide, Dropbox, and many other services are free if you are not a heavy user. That is the ones you will want to find. They take the risk of *betting on your future*. One could even argue that it is a fair deal for them too because the very small customers are willing to pay very little anyway and consume overproportional amounts of resources compared to the big ones. For Dropbox, the administrative efforts required for a low-intensity user are practically identical to an everyday heavy user with a 100 GB account. So companies strive to find ways of dealing with the small customers as efficiently as possible without repelling them.

When was the last time you bought a car? Did you take it out for a test-drive before? Test-drives are so important in our culture that one of the first PC race games was actually called "Test Drive."[13] Some of you might still remember how you could wreck your windshield by simply overpowering your engine.

We are faced with all sorts of trial temptations. Even though we are told that it's not going to be free forever, we act as if it was. Test-drives at car dealerships, shareware that allows us to use software for 30 days, discounted trial periods for AT&T U-verse, sampling food in the supermarket, or even virtual trials such as online configurators. Not seen an online configurator before? Go to any major car manufacturer's website and click on "Build Your Own." Also to this group belong extended return policies and multi-tier offers that suggest you can always return something or change to a plan that is more suitable if you should realize that you don't need

---

[13] Accolade Inc. 1987.

the premium one. Remember those 500 cable TV channels? Do you really need them all? Chances are, like most people, you will never scale back, partly due to convenience and in part due to the reasons given below.

They all appeal to the previously discussed *ownership fallacy* that ultimately works against you. You are eased into something knowing that you can always just walk out the door. Yet once you hold it in your hand, the game changes dramatically. You start building an ever so subtle emotional relationship that giving it up will be hard. So hard that you might rather purchase it or pay too much for it than parting without it.

Michael I. Norton, Daniel Mochon, and Dan Ariely coined the term "Ikea effect" for overvaluing what you have (partially) built yourself, whether it is your furniture, your vintage car, or your business. Building something makes you feel even more ownership than merely owning something. Configurators are the perfect way of exploiting this. You get all the results without actually ever touching the real thing. I have configured BMWs and parked them in my virtual garage since they first had a configurator in the late '90s, I think. And the one time I have seriously overpaid for something in recent history — well, that was my car, even though (or particularly) because it was pre-owned.

Clever sellers know and will let you try.

Right now, make a vow not to participate in any trials anymore unless you have previously made your purchase decision, and the sole remaining task is to

Jan Dominik Gunkel

verify the advertised functions of the product or service.

Free beyond Money

We rave for the free. Giving out stuff without getting any money in return happens to be a rather unsustainable business model for most companies. Enter the stage, marketing. And with it, calorie-free beer, fat-free candy, sodium-free potato chips, and much more. These products are an amazing way to make money. The effect of the word *free* works consistently — irrespective of what if refers to. Sometimes I think we are on our way to a brain-free world.

Since we gravitate to these products, they can often be sold at a premium without reducing demand.

This works so well that we are faced with a glut of something-free products. You can easily validate this by asking your grandma how many products had labels like those when she was young. Then go to the supermarket and start counting. Awhile back, I have even seen a water bottle advertising "fat-free" spring water. Well, the packaging certainly differentiated it from its competition, but in the end, it was still water. No water should contain any fat and thus warrant a fat-free price premium.

While this is not a medical guidebook on nutrition, just ask yourself the next time you are facing a "free of ..." label if that is really good for you and if you really want to buy it.

Key Points to Remember

- *Free* is the hottest emotional hot button there is. Train yourself to resist. Everything comes at a price; sometimes it is simply hidden.
- *Hidden cost* might be time, paying to get access to the offer, experiencing physical pain or guilt, losing your privacy, and getting addicted to something that will cost money in the future.
- *Free trials* invoke the ownership bias, and thus, once you try, you will want to buy. Therefore, your decision to try something should be as solid as a purchasing decision.

Discounts

"Ready for a shock?
I do not use Groupon, Living Social, or any of those lifestyle couponing websites. Trust me, I've heard from all my friends how awesome it is to get a 2 for 1 dinner coupon, a free eye exam, or $20 off a haircut at a salon but …
I do not dine out, my eye exams are covered by insurance, I do not pay more than $15 for a haircut, and I cannot afford most of the lifestyle items they are discounting.
In fact, I do not even look at these websites because I know I'd be tempted to purchase stuff I did not need because it was on sale."
—Beks (2011)

We encounter all sorts of discounts on any day at the mall. Social coupons like Groupon are only the latest flavor of an ever more confusing world. Confusing, really? In a recent behavior study, it was found that more consumers bought a bundle of an ordinary snack with a sophisticated candy for a price X with $2 off than a control group that was offered the whole bundle for only $2. And that held even when X minus $2 was considerably more than $2. So let us check into some flavors of discounts.

Coupons

What is the last coupon that you have used? There are a ton of them in the mail every day. Free coupons that lure you into the supermarket, to Amazon.com, or to any other store. Chances are that we spend a lot of time browsing the coupons—remember your one-hour rule—and finally going to a store that we would not have frequented otherwise. While we are there, we buy much more than we have originally intended. A chain reaction you can only stop at the beginning by throwing all those coupons into the trash right away.

Among consumers, 81% use coupons regularly; 3.5 billion coupons were redeemed by US consumers in 2011 with a total amount of $4.6 billion saved. That is a total value of $1.31 per coupon. But the statistics does not tell us how much more was spent that should have been saved.

When times are bad, we love our coupons. The percentage of people in the United States using coupons for their holiday shopping has increased from 22% to 37% from 2007 to 2011. Consider this. Based on the one-hour rule, even at minimum wage, a $1.31 savings would mean you need to find a coupon at least once every 10 minutes. However, there is a caveat. If you are earning minimum wage, you are probably not interested in the $50 coupon for $600 luggage set, so your average coupon value is much lower. Thus you have even less time to spend to find each coupon. If you are a median wage earner, you earn more than twice the minimum wage. That leaves you with less than 5 minutes to find a coupon. If you are an average earner, you make three to four times minimum wage and thus have only 2–3 minutes to spend on clipping one coupon.

By now, I hope you are convinced that working through coupon books and leaflets is not a worthwhile habit. But how can you still benefit from coupons? First, ask yourself if what you are looking for is worth getting a discount for. There are probably 20% of the items you purchase where you can get 80% of the savings from. The remaining 80% you will do fine if you just consciously spend your money. That already frees 80% of your couponing time. I suggest you use that time to either make money or enjoy life. For the 20% I recommend searching for coupons online. Google will always point you to the sites that offer your item the cheapest, and then it can also find things like "Bestbuy Coupon." Try your luck when buying an expensive digital camera or the like. I recently bought a pair of designer swim trunks at bluefly.com. A quick Google search had retrieved a $5 off coupon code. Took me less than 30 seconds. That's an hourly rate of $600!

Breaking and Slipping Coupons

Coupons as a device to draw us into stores were discussed above. For store owners, there is another even more significant advantage of the coupon folly. Can you guess? Let us start with an experiment. Browse all the coupons you have at this time. How many are past their expiration date?

My parents bought this restaurant coupon book as they wanted to try out new places. Guess what. Once they had the book, they realized there are other restaurants out there they were much more interested in. Finally, the whole thing expired without them eating in any of those places even once.

Airline miles expire, credits in many online and prepaid accounts expire, mail-in rebates expire or get lost. This is most mind-boggling in the case of rebate checks: they are sent out but never cashed. Ouch! The effect is called slippage among trade professionals and a great secondary benefit to store owners.

Or we try to redeem them only to find that the forms are so complicated that we make a mistake and our reward is declined. This effect is called breakage.

In total, a staggering 40% of all rebates and coupons are never redeemed because of those two effects! These account for about $2 billion in extra revenue for retailers and suppliers per year. TiVo, for instance, was able to turn a $857,000 loss into a $9.1. million profit in part by earning $5 from many customers who did not send in their mail-in rebates in Q4/2004.

So how do you stack up? In fact, as I write this, I notice an expired Amazon.com voucher that I am using as bookmark. Another one. The 40% seems to be true for me. Even with the little couponing I do. This is why some call it a "tax on the disorganized."[14]

The good news is that this is a tax you can evade without punishment or immorality! It is your choice to be in the other 60% and take your slice of the pie.

Therefore, persist even if the coupon is expired. And it actually works. You just need to collect your guts and ask, ask again, even ask for the manager if you need to. Don't take no for an answer right away. Most people will not dare ask, and store employees

---

[14] Grow, Brian (2005).

will usually quickly give in after the initial no if they can. If not, it is time to ask for the manager. Please remember, you can be determined and friendly. It is never the store employee's fault. She did not make those rules. Another way of evading this tax is of course you getting organized in the first place.

After all this, you must wonder, why do we love coupons and mail-in rebates so much? A possible behavioral explanation at least for mail-in rebates could be that they provide a *silver lining* on the horizon after a huge expense. You have spent a lot, but you know that you will get something in return later. That sweetens the deal. This is mental accounting fooling us all over again. In reality, only the effective money paid should count.

Pay for Discount

Some coupons we have to buy. The value proposition is literally getting hundreds of dollars in value for a few bucks. Sometimes it is worth it; often it is not. I have this memory of my high school friend Sven. We went to visits friends of my parents in New York City back in the '90s. First time Big Apple. (Oh man, it was big and busy. Bustling with people. Excursions were fun, especially without cell phones to locate each other.) One day, our hosts had sent us to this amazing factory outlet shopping outside the city. (At the time, they weren't as commonplace as they are today.) To make our day, they had given us the coupon book they had bought the last time. Of course they told us how valuable it was. Worth hundreds of dollars. No mention of the actual purchase price, which I guess was about $5 or $10. Since I did not have a particular interest in shopping at that age, my friend Sven was entrusted with the book. After a few stores and a few bags on his hands later, he asked me something that made the alarm bells sound in my head: "Dominik, do you have the coupon book?" Of course I did not have it. I never had it all along. The rest of the afternoon can be summarized by picturing two high school kids frantically searching a factory outlet center the size of Lower Manhattan for a coupon book "worth hundreds of dollars" and thinking of excuses to our hosts. Maybe that's how I came to hate coupons.

The most explicit are store clubs that get you discounts for an annual fee. Like Douglas fragrance store chain in Europe. Membership gets you a €5 coupon for your birthday, but you pay €12 to be part of the club. To give them some credit, they also send you their magazine once a quarter or so, and they promise to give you nicer samples in the store with your purchases. Is there anything better for retail than consumers actually paying to receive advertising and samples?

Or consider the GNC Gold Club. A pretty exclusive-sounding way to extract more revenue from you. You pay $15 to get 20% off on purchases during the first seven days of the month. Of course it can be worth it.

Do you really buy all your nutrients in the first week of each month? I would say it is possible but tough. Knowing that supplements are a high-margin business, there are probably other ways for you to find even better deals. Consider online and save some sales tax on top. But that's not the main point. Just as in the case of "free," there are hidden costs involved. What you are really doing here is selling them permission to spam you. More temptation will be in the mail, and we all know how we react to coupons. To avoid temptation, I have made it a rule only to fall for these kinds of deals when it saves me some real money with the first purchase I make, and I always use a fake address.

Based on behavioral research, we hunt for deals. We are even willing to pay for them — irrespective of the actual need. So unless you are the inventor of self-discipline, the best rule of thumb is skip buying coupons altogether. We are simply overconfident when we choose them, and there are thousands of reasons why we let them expire. Here is a quote I love about buying at Groupon and Living Social: "Our Groupon lives, in which, in pursuit of bargains, we settle for things we kind of maybe would consider owning. Services we might maybe someday use. We compete for crap at 60% off."[15]

Free's Little Brother — Half Off

Short story: Even after a few years, I still wear two pairs of Ralph Lauren Polo Sport sneakers — a black and a brown one — quite frequently. Why do I tell you? Because I got the second half off. To be honest, I wouldn't have bought the first if it wouldn't have been for that deal. Maybe out of a sense of guilt, I started

---

[15] Davide Granger (2011).

wearing them, and now I wear them out of habit. Consequentially, this was a pretty good investment for me. But the better investment would have been to buy just one pair — the brown one I really like!

I am sure you have seen quite a few "half off" promotions. Their effect is considerably weaker than that of a free tag. Yet it is still noticeable. I would advise any retailer to stick with free or rephrasing half off to free wherever possible for maximum effect. For instance, "Buy one get one free" is essentially the same as "Buy two at half off."

For consumers, first thing to remember is "half off" is a trick just as "free." Second thing, "half off" often comes in promotions, where you have to purchase multiple units. Whether free or half-off chocolate, if you are fighting obesity, it might not be a treat. Instead, it comes at a hidden cost as discussed above in the free section. Or that expiring yoghurt that comes at 50% off if you buy a 12-pack. Well, how much yoghurt can you eat today without throwing up?

Employee Discounts

Once I had this colleague who had a friend at a very large Detroit motor company. He announced that he had just bought his new vehicle with a huge employee discount, and as I was certainly going to buy a car too; his friend could help me with that as well. Usually, the only cars I buy are made in Spartanburg, South Carolina, but this employee discount had tickled my interest. So I did some digging. Well, I found a study conducted by researchers of my alma mater, the University of California at Berkeley, and the MIT. It showed that many cars could have been purchased at a lower price outside the program than with the employee discount. This held true for all three Detroit automakers. Apparently, all the people needed to hear was that they were getting a good — as well as access restricted — price, and so they believed.

Charm Prices

If you are amazed by the effect of free, you are going to love the second low-cost focal point: 99 cents. Have you ever heard of Dave Gold? He was the one who made a fortune finding out about it. In his little California liquor store, he realized that selling some wine at 99¢ increased sales for all liquor in his store, even wine previously sold at 79¢. Years later, he went on to start the first 99¢ store, and many followed. Do you know another famous "99¢ store"? Apple iTunes and App Store. Steve Jobs fought music industry executives quite a bit for the 99¢ per song. History has proven him right.

Next time you enter a dollar store or iTunes, remember you are a deer walking into a machine gun fire. You will get hit.

Charm prices are prices that have an appeal simply because of their looks. The 99¢ above are one of the strongest charm prices. Generally, prices with a 9 in the end tip the scales in favor of buying. We even buy stuff with a price ending on a 9 that we would not have bought at a lower price. In doubt? A $39 sweater in a mail order catalog was purchased more often than it was sold in control groups where it was priced at \$34 or \$44.

However, this effect is fairly small and easily superseded by others, such as a sale cue. As this effect is widely known, today pretty much all prices end on 9¢. Some stores have even progressed to prices ending in 7 or 5, but to date there is no evidence of that being effective. What does that mean for us? Don't worry too much about general charm prices. Only with larger items that end in \$9 or \$90, it's probably worthwhile to be a little cautious.

The Discount You Really Want

Every dollar saved has the same value. It does not matter whether you save \$10 of a bouquet of flowers that was tagged at \$50 or of a \$500 laptop. In both cases, you saved \$10. This sounds pretty clear, but we usually do not act this way.

Imagine you are out to buy a calculator—like the one you probably used at school. Daniel Kahnemann ran this experiment a while ago. He found that we would rather save \$5 on a \$15 calculator than \$5 on one for \$125. While the percentage gain in the first case is certainly larger, there is no reason we should make an effort any larger than the one we would go through for saving \$5 on the more expensive one. Saving \$5 is of equal benefit in both cases, and you should get it where you can unless the hassle of obtaining it supersedes its benefits.

In a more complicated setting, Kahnemann added another product to the bundle so the total in each store would come out to \$140 or to \$135 after the discount.

Funny enough, we would still act in the same irrational way. If the cheap item got the discount, we would drive across town to get it. For the expensive item, participants could not care less. Remember in both stores the total came out to $135. Apparently, not all $5 seem to be created equal. In our perception, it depends on which item is discounted.

Do not let yourself be tricked into going to another store just because they offer low-price items at discount levels. You can probably save even more on the big stuff.

Another bummer. Oftentimes you will not be able to find a discount offer on the product you want. Why not make your own? Ask for a discount. I know this takes some guts. If you are a little timid, ask yourself, *When was the last time you read about a store manager ripping out a customer's guts after he asked for a discount?* If you can't remember any occurrences, then maybe— just maybe—it is not that dangerous after all. You can do it—with a smile on your face. And you can only win. If she says no, you can still pay full price and enjoy the product.

How much discount is realistic? You want to make sure that you have a good chance of winning the deal. Of course this varies from setting to setting. I always start with 20% of the market price, which I have found to be an effective strategy. Market price in this case means the lowest generally available street price, which might quite likely be an offer from a different store. For high-tech and other known low-margin products, I am less aggressive; and for software and other high-margin products, I ask for even more. In the end, it is up to you how much you are willing to yield. With time, you will get better and better. As I elaborated in the chapter on differentiation, I once bought a custom-made set of exquisite brand dining room furniture for $13,000 that was originally quoted at $22,300. That is a whopping 42%. (Oh, and after I had negotiated that, I opted to buy an additional set, which I privately resold, further sweetening the deal for me.)

My friend Anne Veling and one of the best hairdressers I know offers 50% off for recommendations to you and the new customer. I really loved this offer when she first told me about it. Credibility is important to me, and I would never recommend anything subpar to my friends. Since she is the best, I do not have an issue with that. We both win. Consequently, I have asked for similar deals in other places myself and got them granted.

Beware though that some sellers might actually not consider you a worthy buyer if you haggle too much. Forgoing a deal with you might have to do with their brand understanding or simply their irrationality.

As a little exercise, I suggest picking a shopping day and asking for a discount everywhere you go. Just make it the rule of the day. And I mean really everywhere, even at the post office. Part of the exercise is getting comfortable asking, part is getting comfortable with startled looks, and so on. Who knows? Maybe you will even get a surprise deal. One suggestion: If they say no, be persistent and ask again with open questions: "How could we make this work/cheaper?" or "What else could you do for me?"

Key Points to Remember

- Coupon clipping is hardly ever worth it. Stop it.
- For those coupons and rebates that you decide to keep, make sure you don't let them expire and turn them in correctly.
- Mail-in rebates and cash-back offers provide a *silver lining* meant to sweeten the deal for you. They fool you into feeling that you are actually getting more than you are. Look at what you are paying.
- Discounts are emotional hot buttons meant to tease you, not necessarily offer with a reduced price. Same with *charm prices*. They are not necessarily exceptionally cheap—they were selected to look their part. Even if an offer looks good, you will want to make a reason-based decision.
- We tend to value discounts as a proportion of the overall purchase price. However, $5 saved on a $10 item has the same value as $5 saved on a $5000 item. The latter will be much easier to negotiate. Do it.
- A discount on a price tag is not a discount. The only real discount is the one you have asked for yourself.

Fooling Around

"Fool! Don't you see now that I could have poisoned you a
hundred times had I been able to live without you."
— Cleopatra
Last Egyptian pharaoh

"You can fool all the people some of the time, and some of the
people all the time, but you cannot fool all the people all the time."
— Abraham Lincoln
Former president of the United States of America

Opaque Offers

I have been wondering for a while why Kroger's
offers a 10 for $10. Then I found out you can actually
buy one item for $1 or any number of items you wish.
So I did a quick study at my Kroger's in Ann Arbor. I
checked what products were running the promotion, in
this case, bottled water and bell peppers. So I asked 20
customers where I could see they had purchased these
two items. It turns out that quite a few of them had
purchased 10. When I asked them why they had
bought 10, all except one replied that they considered
this part of the promotion and thought they had to buy

10. Judging by the rest of the items in their cart, they hardly needed 10 bell peppers right now . . . but Kroger's sold them.

When was the last time you saw a promotion that was not entirely clear based on its tagline?

Opaque Prices

Sometimes prices are not evident in their true amount right away. On occasion, you might only learn the true price after your purchase. Watch out for those. But it also works the other way round. You might only know what you get after you have paid.

On one of my trips to Chicago, where I like to stay in five-star hotels on Michigan Avenue but do not really want to afford it, I used hotwire.com. Hotwire is a service that lets you book a hotel by the neighborhood, the star rating, and a few more criteria for a supercheap price. However, the name is obscured until you have paid. Once you use Hotwire regularly in a certain area, you will know with stunning certainty what properties are offered. So that time, I had once more chosen my favorite five-star hotel for $69. Imagine vintage skyscraper right on Michigan Avenue. Since like most hotels this one belongs to a chain and I use the lower-end hotels of that chain quite a bit, I usually get a free upgrade at their properties due to my status. During check-in, I casually ask, and the clerk tells me, "Let me check." Moments later, she hands me the keys, and I am curious to see the last two digits being "00." While I am getting ready to turn around, she mentions something about ... "elevator." My first thought was, *I know where the elevator is*. Then I realize she said "private elevator." So I inquire again and learn that I have a private elevator. All right, "00" and "private elevator"! Maybe I am the new James Bond. Guess what. I took my elevator up to the 40th floor or something and stepped out into my floor — my room. They had just assigned me an entire floor. Windows on all four sides overlooking the entire city and a bathroom the "size of the Blue Banana," to quote Julia Roberts in *Pretty Woman*.

That's what can hide behind an opaque price. Play with the right ones often enough, and you can strike it big. Similar opportunities wait on sites like priceline.com.

A side note on upgrades on airlines, hotels, and the like. There are no bulletproof ways of ensuring an upgrade everywhere anytime, but you can do a quick web search to find some tips. This way, you can hope to get a decent percentage of your trips upgraded. Not doing this is simply a waste.

Remain a Skeptic

Our brain loves the word *because*. We consciously ask for a reason, and our subconscious is satisfied with any reason — just as long as there appears to be one. Even in negotiations, we tend to agree more if the other side gives a reason. Those reasons might be as silly as and self-referencing as "May I use the Xerox machine, because I have to make copies?"

So if you hear a reason for a price increase or for a high price, question that reason. You might hear a somewhat more elaborate "We had to increase prices for the cabbage by 20% because of the long rainy season in Florida this year." Well, the rain in Florida does not really have much to do with cabbage prices, but people tend to accept it.

Key Points to Remember

- Some offers are simply not clear. Don't buy them just because you think this is how the promotion works. Ask.
- When prices are not shown, great deals can be found and a lot of money can be wasted. It is worth exploring.
- Remain a skeptic, especially when you hear "because."

MAKING IT HAPPEN

In this part ...

You have already mastered most of the theoretical aspects. Now it is time to ensure you make the changes you want. Let's push the envelope together with seven proven behavioral techniques that will lead you far beyond this book and into your richer future. Graduation time!

Making It Happen

"The price of inaction is far greater than the cost of making a mistake."
— Meister Eckhart
13th-century European theologian

"You will never change your life until you change something you do daily."
— Mike Murdock
American televangelist

What You Have Learned

In the dense chapters above, you have learned precisely how irrational we all are. Now, you know dozens of biases and fallacies as well as what they mean for your financial and personal situation. You hold the keys to benefit from this knowledge. You have become an expert on pricing and will now successfully conduct any negotiation. Some of the learnings might even help you advance in your job, with your family or other personal matters.

Most of our lives are intertwined with those of others. Our action impacts other people, and other people make us react. We may think we know the solution, but our solution will be much more valuable if we work with each other to implement it instead of simply exploiting each other. So talk to your partner and friends about this. Tell them what you have learned and what you are up to. It is said that we remember 10% of what we learn but 90% of what we teach.

When pointing out something specific, watch out not to invalidate any feelings. The others are not stupid but just as smart as you and maybe simply unaware of their own irrationalities. Feel free to gently introduce them to this book or other articles on the subject. A good life is not about outsmarting your mates with behavioral economics but living a great life together, where you all understand each other. Use your sparring partners. You can be an amazing tag team to conquer the world.

"This Time It's Different."

You have read this book, and this time you will really do the things advised and change. Yeah, really! Really?

Let me tell you about the "This time it's different"[16] bias with a little story—and maybe, just maybe, this is a story about you. Say you bought stocks of Amazon.com and many other amazing new economy stocks back in the late '90s, the heyday of the new Internet economy. Amazon.com at the time was losing money, and it was questionable if they would ever turn

---

[16] Rogov, Kenneth and Carmen M. Reinhart (2011).

a profit, yet they were valued at more than $28.46 billion in the fourth quarter of 1999. That was more than 18 times the value of the profitable and established Barnes & Noble, Inc., which was valued at about $1.55 billion at the time. You were totally convinced that this was a new era. Things were different. Profit did not matter anymore. Not even sales mattered anymore. All you needed was a website, and you were in for the ride. Centuries ago, there were the railway bubble, a tulip bubble, and the Great Depression. This was different. Totally so.

In Q4/2001, Amazon.com was valued at $3.39 billion — almost a 10th of what it was worth two years before. People had to declare personal bankruptcy and lost all their retirement savings. You were "lucky" and just lost a lot of money. What did you learn?[17]

It didn't take 10 years after for us to see the housing bubble inflate and burst.

If one thing is true, it is that some things do not change. There are fundamental rules, and no matter how hard we wish for, they are not going away — at least not for long. And they always come back with a vengeance.

When you look back at past attempts to change your life, you might find that you always reverted to the old you — the fat you, the poor you, the unsatisfied you.

Therefore, let us now discuss some further tricks for you to actually make the change. Here is what has worked for me in the order of success. Thanks to all the

---

[17] Market caps pulled from http://www.wikinvest.com/ on Oct. 3, 2012.

people who have figured these out. This time it can be different. Really!

1. Using Your Powers Wisely

Have you realized that there are times of the day when you are especially weak and prone to do anything but the right thing? Getting up is really tough for me. But once I am out of bed, I can go to the office and prepare my daily list of chores. No matter how evil they might be, I am able and willing to address them. However, when I get home, I have a hard time to pack my bag and go to the gym or write that letter to my aunt thanking her for my birthday present. Sounds familiar?

This effect is called *ego depletion*. Willpower is like a battery. After you have relaxed or slept, it is full and you can change the world. Following a rough day, it's empty and you can't really control yourself anymore. Possibly you have even found yourself in periods of extended stress, where one night of sleep or taking a walk couldn't restore it much.

To maintain my battery well, I found four things to be helpful: In a state of maximum charge, I make sure to set myself up to accomplish what needs to be done during the entire day, and then I simply go on autopilot. Typically this happens in the morning. And as for the getting-up part, I have recorded my favorite song with a voice-over increasingly shouting me out of bed. It's what it takes for me. Then I take a solid one-minute ice-cold shower before breakfast. After that, I feel like nothing can stop me. If you can will yourself to do this, you can do anything. I mean what is going to be worse than an ice-cold morning shower? (Additional benefit: The shower ritual burns a serious bunch of calories.)

Second, I take a 5–15 minute break every 90 minutes when working. Sounds like a waste of time? I dare you to try it. It will greatly improve your performance and creativity. Unfortunately, however, if you work in any sort of standardized process, this might not be possible. You can't just not affix doors to cars as they pass by on the conveyer belt.

Third, I make sure glucose levels in my blood are high enough. We might automatically do this. Remember how we used to eat chocolate while we studied for school? Unfortunately, this is a catch-22 as it will make you fat despite the cold showers. But if you eat and exercise, you can be in shape and have sufficient glucose in your blood.

Fourth, I let go. Relaxing means not just lying around but just doing what comes to my mind. No (or very little) questions asked.

This way, you can build a reservoir of willpower allowing you to achieve whatever you want, instead of shooting for a burn-out syndrome as you constantly underperform to your own expectations. More on this can be found in Roy Baumeister's *Willpower: Rediscovering the Greatest Human Strength.*

2. Overcoming Procrastination and Twin-crastination

Procrastination is your toughest enemy. How do you win this battle?

Know your tendencies. I know someone who built and ran a multibillion-dollar company. He would never start preparing anything until the last hour. Yet he knew this and had thus got a highly-qualified secretary of the opposite traits. She made sure to allot the right time slots in advance and to push him as necessary. Deadlines can be of great help. So set some specific ones and stick to them. As you do that, space them so you have enough room to achieve whatever needs to be done in between.

Moreover, I have a goal plan for each year. Each quarter or month, there are new things I aim to introduce into my life. For example, I know I need to be extremely fit for skiing once winter rolls around — especially in some muscle groups that are hardly used in the summer. Therefore, my dedicated workout begins "on November 1 after work." It does not start "in the fall" or "sometime prior to skiing season," but at a precisely specified time.

How about turning the table on procrastination? This is the mother of all cheats if used correctly: Have two equally beneficial tasks and use them to procrastinate from each other! I use writing this book as a way to procrastinate from exercising and exercising as a way to procrastinate from writing. My body is in the best shape ever. You be the judge for the book. This is what I call "twincrastination." But be warned, using this technique will easily allow bad habits to creep into your life.

3. Default to Desired Action

We are habit driven. Without a conscious effort, we revert to the default, and that default is usually the past status quo. Therefore, we have to create an environment that makes the desired action the easy solution. Remember escalating commitment and self-herding.

You can do so, for instance, by sending money to your savings account automatically once you get the paycheck. Of course you can always get it back, but chances are you won't. Even after years of research and experiment, I still use this to trick and send half my paycheck to savings. (Sounds like a lot. I thought so too. But it works.)

If you can't imagine saving today, make creative use of procrastination by committing to forced savings in the future: Once you have calculated how much money you need every month to cover your costs and how much you have left over, decide how much you want to save. Instead of putting it into your savings account manually every month starting today, create an autotransfer in your account starting the month after next and add an additional 10% savings. It will not hurt you today, and I bet Future You will manage.

4. Prevent Undesired Action

Governments put people in prison so they don't do bad stuff. I am not suggesting you lock yourself away. But why not get rid of stuff that is bad for you? Or block access to it?

You are spending tons of money at Starbucks? How about making it a habit to take a coffee from home to work. There are beautiful reusable cups available, and with that cup in the car, you probably will not stop at the Starbucks drive-through as your cup holder is already full.

If you generally drink too much, stop having large quantities of alcohol around the house. If only one can of Bud is in the fridge, you just cannot drink more. Better still, keep it in the basement. If you have to walk that far to get one, I am sure you will think twice.

Define spending limits for yourself: If you can't do without Starbucks, how about getting one of those prepaid Starbucks cards (do not activate the autorecharge feature). Define how much you are going to spend there per week. Trust me, I am still tempted.

Getting rid of your credit card is not a realistic option, but if you are tempted to shop on impulse, leave it at home and bring just the right amount of cash. If you have to return home to get the card before you can buy that new dress from the window at Neiman Marcus, you should have enough time to cool off and control your impulses.

Are e-mail and Facebook your big time sinks preventing you from getting anything else accomplished? Make it a habit to close your mail client and Facebook once you are done. Sometimes I find myself hitting Alt+Tab to switch to mail. When it's not there, I remember that I do not want to do e-mail more than once a day. Also, disable pop-up notifications about new e-mails and new Facebook info on your computer, cell phone, and iPad. If something is truly urgent, people will call you. Doing this is the single greatest time saver ever. There are 24 hours each day; use them to accomplish something that makes you happy. As I once heard, "Time passes anyway; we might as well do something useful."

5. Take Small Steps
If you try to flip your entire life in a breeze, you might "succeed" for a few days, but then rebound to being your old self afterward. By changing one small thing at a time instead, you will have an easier time consciously controlling it. A small activity regularly

monitored and built into a habit is your first step to the top of the mountain. Many of these small steps will get you there.

But also know when to take a leap. In discussions with many friends, I found that people differ in this respect. When I set out to write this book, I was extremely motivated and set out to do it with the ambitious goal of finishing it in three months. I completely immersed myself into writing and basically completed 90% of the raw text within six weeks while traveling in Argentina and Hawaii. That is not exactly a small step—especially while exploring an unfamiliar geography at the same time. I know that I am part of the lucky group that can do big things in concentrated efforts. Other full-time writers I know write a page per day. But no matter how you do it. Both can lead you to the top of your mountain. Pick the strategy that works for you and stick with it.

6. Raise the Issue to a Conscious Decision

In this book, you have seen that our subconscious is the cornerstone of most decisions in life. But this "does not prove that consciousness never does anything," according to Roy Baumeister, professor of psychology at the Florida State University, in the *New York Times*. "It is rather like showing you can hot-wire a car to start the ignition without keys. That is important and potentially useful information, but it does not prove that keys do not exist or that keys are useless."[18] The purpose of this book was to teach us how to make sure we use those keys. One of the keys could be little reminders from your past and future.

---

[18] Carey, Benedict (2007).

They can guide you to lead the life you really want. Let me explain:

Awhile back, I flew out to California to take an amazing communications workshop with Dr. Mark Rittenberg, a former theater director. At the end of the highly emotional class, he had us write a letter to him from the perspective of our future selves one year ahead. (If you ever get a chance to work with him, make sure you do so.) What good was that? Essentially, it would serve as a reminder to ourselves next year. We will see what we aspired to be. Also, writing it down raised the issue to our consciousness already today. Since we were supposed to mail this letter to someone else, the commitment is even stronger, as you will see in the next section.

Accordingly, you can put this book or a reminder Post-it with the following questions on your bedside and on your breakfast table. You might even want to write the answers into a diary, and bonus, you will be amazed when you pick up your old diary again five years from now.

- Before sleep, ask the following questions:
  - In what three instances did behavecon improve my life today?
  - In what three instances did I get fooled by behavecon today?
  - What would I do differently if I lived this day again?
  - What have I learned today that I can apply later?
- During breakfast, ask the following:
  - Where do I plan to apply behavecon today?
  - What dangers do I expect today that I can counter with behavecon?

- Who can I teach about behavecon today?

Finding answers to these questions will prove staggeringly difficult in the beginning. The more and more you do it though, the easier it will become. You will start hardwiring this new understanding into your mind. My experience with several test subjects I have coached in the past showed that, over time, as you get into the above bedtime/morning ritual, your mind will automatically ask—and answer—those questions during the day.

Accept the answers even though they might be unpleasant because they show your mistakes. Embrace them as an opportunity to improve. Here is an example.

Last time I was in San Francisco, I strolled around one of the downtown malls killing a day. At some point, I popped into a Crumpler store on Market Street. Oh, what lovely bags they had. As I am an avid photographer, I am always annoyed that bringing the right gear is such a hassle. They offered several camera bags. After toying a little with them, I ended up purchasing two. They both seemed useful to specific occasions. Out of the store, as I walked the city streets again, I started thinking (which of course I should have been doing before) and justifying that I needed those two bags. I was falling into a trap of confirmation bias looking for arguments confirming my decision. Clearly, one of those bags was enough. I couldn't realistically see myself repacking my gear among three bags depending on the occasion. (I already had one at home.) So I took a deep breath and returned to the store despite that the clerk had already removed the tags from the bag. My mind started preparing for the discussions as to why I had to return it and what had happened to all the tags ... Once I got there—somewhat out of my comfort zone—I made my plea. No questions asked, I got my money back.

This had several benefits. I saved about $45, it protected me from having some more junk around the house, and most significantly, it expanded my comfort zone for acknowledging my mistakes and fixing them. Especially the latter can be huge. I am sure you don't like to be wrong either.

You can also employ the strategy of placing Post-its to remind you of something in the specific places, where that activity needs to be accomplished. For instance, on my kitchen cabinet, it says "workout" to remind me to exercise before each meal. It works amazingly well. The effect eventually wears off, as you brain considers the note to be part of the usual environment and doesn't bother anymore. By then, however, you should already have formed the habit.

I realized this when a visiting friend asked me about the note, which had been hanging there for quite a while unnoticed. So I took it down as I didn't need it anymore. If you realize that you don't see your note anymore and have not built a persisting habit yet, check the placing of the Post-it or get a different color. Red works great—especially on men.

Another example on how to raise something to a level of consciousness is found at http://www.acomplaintfreeworld.org. This group, which is trying to make the world better by making us stop complaining, uses a simple trick. All followers of the cause get a wristband. By physically changing the arm for the bracelet each time you complain, you make your subconscious behavior conscious and thus make learning possible. For this to work, you need to notice that you are complaining. Here too the band helps: Putting it on, as well as all the people inquiring about it, primes you to notice complaining. Voila!

7. Punish and Reward Yourself/Make It a Game

There are a few ways how you can gamify your quest. If you are a player, this might work well for you.

Commit yourself to others by announcing to your buddies what you are going to do. Cheating them will feel worse than just cheating yourself. For example, tell your friends to ask you 6 months down the road if you still have that autotransfer you created above. That way, you will not just cancel it.

Create a spreadsheet, pin it to your fridge or bedroom wall, and visualize progress for you to see all the time. Checking your net worth or any other relevant metric every day can also become a game. Add certain targets and rewards that you issue to yourself. Say, after saving $1K, spend $100 on some truly exhilarating experience. That will make it much easier to hit your next target in the long run.

Modern ways are offered by websites such as bloggingawaydebt.com or lifekraze.com. The latter makes you microblog to commit yourself. There, you can collect badges for achieving your goals. I have never used any of these new forms, but I could see that it might help. If you have a competitive spirit, adding some competition might serve you well.

Typically, financials are something that are oftentimes not discussed among friends, but why not compete with your spouse for a common goal? (Warning: Don't play who can afford the biggest car on the street with your neighbors.)

If you do better with the stick than the carrot, how about automatically punishing yourself for misbehavior. For that savings plan, for example, you could sign up for a plan that costs you a huge penalty if you cancel it prematurely. If you do so, do not let it run for too long — maybe a year or so — as your life circumstances might actually change for really forcing yourself to pay the fine that might make you even worse.

What's Next?

In the end, I want to leave you with a tantalizing quote from one of my former landlords referring to personal finance: "I am certain with something so important to your life you are an expert yourself." With that, he flattered me and screwed me over as I signed the overpriced lease, foolheartedly falling into this very trap. He certainly was an expert; I admire him for that in spite of his twisted values. The gently nagging pain for the years to come was one of the inspirations for this book. And for you, this is to illustrate that you can learn from anyone, no matter who they are and/or how incompatible their value set is with yours. Go, keep pushing the envelope and find more books, blogs, and people to glean some knowledge from.

I hope I have inspired at least a few thoughts that will help you get closer to becoming the person you desire to be. If I have been successful, you have learned a lot — about life, money, and especially about yourself and other people. So before we move on, may I ask you to abide by what you have learned and spread the word to others. This will make the world a better place for all of us. And if you have any feedback, I appreciate you letting me know via the book's website.

Key Points to Remember

This time it can be different. You can change with these steps:
- Treat your willpower battery with due care.
- Overcome procrastination by using your willpower wisely and twincrastinate.
- Make the desired action your default.
- Prevent undesired activities.
- Take small steps.
- Raise relevant issues to conscious attention.
- Make it a game.

Still there? Good! Before I let you off the hook, please take a sheet of paper and a pen and turn off your cell for 5-10 minutes. Go ahead and write a letter to yourself. What is it that you have learned in this book, and what would you like to achieve in the next five years? Put it into an envelope, seal it, and put it away. Maybe a little reminder in your calendar would do good, so you find the letter in five years.

BIBLIOGRAPHY

Sources

"The only true wisdom is in knowing you know nothing."
—Socrates
Classical Greek philosopher

Sources are listed in alphabetical order per chapter. If you feel anything is misquoted or any source lacks representation, please let me know. Thank you.

Chapter: You, Your Life, and This Book

Beyer, S. (2012). "Ich denke, also irre ich," *Der Spiegel*, 14/2012, April 2, 2012.

Dworschak, M. (2012). "Zaubertrank der Zuversicht," *Der Spiegel*, 1/2012, pp. 116–125.

Eagleman, D. (2011). "Incognito: The Secret Lives of the Brain."

Seligman, M. E. P. (1991). "To the Optimists Will Go the World," *Los Angeles Times*, Sept. 27, 1991.

Nielsen (2012). "Holiday Shopping," in: Inc. Dec. 2011/Jan. 2012, p. 32.

Stanley, T. J., and W. D. Danko (2010). "The Millionaire Next Door: The Surprising Secrets of America's Wealthy."

Stiglitz , J. E. (2010). Freefall: America, Free Markets, and the Sinking of the World Economy.

Movie. "The Joneses," D. Borte, 2009.

Chapter: Your Assets

Ariely, D. (2008). "Predictably Irrational: The Hidden Forces That Shape Our Decisions."

Byrne, R. (2006). "The Secret."

Carmon, Z. and D. Ariely (2000). "Focusing on the Forgone: How Value Can Appear so Different to Buyers and Sellers," *Journal of Consumer Research*, vol. 27 (3), Dec. 2000, 360–370.

Gupta, S. (2011). "Es ist möglich, komplett vom Containern zu leben." Aug. 8, 2011, retrieved at http://www.kinofenster.de/film-des-monats/archiv-film-des-monats/kf1109/hanna-poddig-kf1109/ on Apr. 29, 2012.

Kahneman, D. (2002). "Autobiography." *Nobelprize.org*, retrieved at http://www.nobelprize.org/nobel_prizes/economics/laureates/2002/kahneman-autobio.html Mar. 27, 2013.

Kivetz, R. (1999). "Advances In Research on Mental Accounting and Reason-Based Choice." *Marketing Letters*, vol. 10 (3), Aug. 1999, 249–266.

Langer, E. J. (1975). "The Illusion of Control," *Journal of Personality and Social Psychology*, vol. 32 (2), Aug. 1975, 311–328.

Lunenburg, F. C. (2010). "Escalation of Commitment: Patterns of Retrospective Rationality," *International Journal of Management, Business, and Administration*, vol. 13 (1), 2010.

Orman, S. (2007). "The Money Book for the Young, Fabulous & Broke."

Taleb, N. N. (2008). "The Black Swan: The Impact of the Highly Improbable."

Thaler, R. H. (1985). "Mental Accounting and Consumer Choice." *Marketing Science* 4, 199–214.

Schubert, F. (2009). "Protest als Lebensform, Frankfurter Rundschau," Oct. 16, 2009, retrieved at http://www.fr-online.de/kultur/buchmesse--nachgefragt-protest-als-lebensform,1472786,2927424.html on Apr. 29, 2012.

Unknown (undated). "Top 10 Crooked CEOs," *TIME*, retrieved Apr. 27, 2012, http://www.time.com/time/specials/packages/articl e/0,28804,1903155_1903156_1903277,00.html

Chapter: Your Income and Spending of Money and Time

Ariely, D. (2012). "The (Honest) Truth about Dishonesty: How We Lie to Everyone — Especially Ourselves."

Aslett, D. (2005). "Clutter's Last Stand."

Beyond Budgeting Roundtable. "Which Organizations Have Become Empowered and Adaptive Organizations?" retrieved at http://www.bbrt.org/beyond-budgeting/bb-bbo.html on Mar. 27, 2013.

Carroll, J., and S. Chun (2008). "'Zero' Chance Lottery Tickets Stun Some Players," *CNN.com*, July 7, 2008, retrieved at http://articles.cnn.com/2008-07-07/us/lottery.tickets_1_top-prizes-paula-otto-scratch-off-ticket?_s=PM:US on Mar. 3, 2012.

Congressional Budget Office (2012). "Report on the Troubled Assets Relief Program," Mar. 2012.

Crosby, D. (2011). "Sex, Funds, & Rock n' Roll," *TEDx Huntsville*, retrieved at http://youtu.be/1kh9nqG8TyA on Oct. 3, 2012.

Dubner, S. J., and S. D. Levitt (2005). "Monkey Business," *New York Times*, June 5, 2005, retrieved at http://www.nytimes.com/2005/06/05/magazine/05 FREAK.html on Aug. 8, 2010.

Fields, J. (2011). "Dust in the Wind?" retrieved from http://www.jonathanfields.com/blog/was-this-your-life/ on Apr. 4, 2011.

Findley, T. S., and F. N. Caliendo (2011). "Interacting Mechanisms of Time Inconsistency," Working Paper, Sept. 21, 2011.

Funny2, Inc. (undated). "The Odds," retrieved at http://www.funny2.com/oddsb.htm on Apr. 29, 2012.

Highbeam Research, Inc. (2009). "Lotteries. Gambling: What's at Stake?" *Encyclopedia.com*, retrieved at http://www.encyclopedia.com/topic/lottery.aspx on Oct. 3, 2012.

Ipsos Public Affairs (2011). "Eight in Ten (83%) PayPal Merchants Say Sales Have Increased Since Offering Popular Payment Method," Press Release (One should note that the study was commissioned by PayPal and there was no control group.)

Jobs, S. (2005): Stanford commencement address, June 12, 2005, retrieved at http://www.guardian.co.uk/technology/2011/oct/09/steve-jobs-stanford-commencement-address on Jan. 13, 2013.

Karinthy, F. (1929). Chain-Links. Translated from Hungarian and annotated by Adam Makkai and Enikö Jankó.

Kivetz, R. (1999). "Advances In Research on Mental Accounting and Reason-Based Choice," *Marketing Letters*, vol. 10 (3), Aug. 1999, 249–266.

Kolay, S., and G. Shaffer (2003). "Bundling and Menus of Two-Part Tariffs," *The Journal of Industrial Economics*, vol. LI (3), Sept. 2003.

Lerner, M. (2012). "What Influence Do Payment Methods Have on Purchasing Habits?" retrieved at http://www.quora.com/Behavioral-Economics/What-influence-do-payment-methods-have-on-purchasing-habits on Oct. 3, 2012.

Philips, K. (2011). "Is It Really That Bad to Be Irrational When It Comes to Economics?" *Deseret News*, Nov. 28, 2011, retrieved at http://www.deseretnews.com/article/700202179/Is-it-really-that-bad-to-be-irrational-when-it-comes-to-economics.html on Mar. 1, 2012.

Porter, E. (2011). "The Price of Everything."

Poundstone, W. (2010). "Priceless: The Myth of Fair Value (and How to Take Advantage of It)."

Prelec, D., and G. Loewenstein (1998). "The Red and the Black: Mental Accounting of Savings and Debt," *Marketing Science*, vol. 17 (1), 4–28.

Roth, J. D. (2012). "The Tyranny of Clutter," *Entrepreneur*, Jan. 2012.

Schwarzenegger, A. (2012). "Total Recall."

Slovic, P., and S. Lichtenstein (1968). "Relative Importance of Probabilities and Payoffs in Risk Taking," *Journal of Experimental Psychology*, vol. 78 (3, pt.2), Nov. 1968, 1–18.

Stiglitz, J. E. (2010). *Freefall: America, Free Markets, and the Sinking of the World Economy.*

Sunstein, C. (2012). "Show Me the Money," retrieved at http://www.tnr.com/print/article/books-

and-arts/magazine/108153/show-me-the-money on Dec. 11, 2012.

Tversky, A. and D. Kahneman (1991). "Loss Aversion in Riskless Choice: A Reference Dependent Model," *Quarterly Journal of Economics*, 106, 1039–1061.

Unknown (2012). "Deutsche Bank statt Ackermann-Bank," *Frankfurter Rundschau*, Sept. 11, 2012.

U.S. Census Bureau, Statistical Abstract of the United States (2012). "Table 1363. Household Net Saving Rates by Country: 1995 to 2008," *International Statistics*, 855.

Chapter: Ambition
Agassi, A. (2010). "Open: An Autobiography."

Ariely, D. (2008). "Predictably Irrational: The Hidden Forces That Shape Our Decisions."

Edmunds.com, Inc. (2010). "Depreciation Infographic: How Fast Does My New Car Lose Value?" Sept. 24, 2010, retrieved at http://www.edmunds.com/car-buying/how-fast-does-my-new-car-lose-value-infographic.html on May 17, 2012.

Gladwell, M. (2007). "Blink: The Power of Thinking without Thinking."

Gladwell, M. (2011). "Outliers: The Story of Success."

Kahneman, D. (2002). "Autobiography." *Nobelprize.org*, retrieved at http://www.nobelprize.org/nobel_prizes/economics/laureates/2002/kahneman-autobio.html on Mar. 27, 2013,.

Kahneman, D. (1994). "New Challenges to the Rationality Assumption," *Journal of Institutional and Theoretical Economics*, 150, 18–36.

Kahneman, D., and A. Tversky (1979). Prospect Theory: An Analysis of Decision Under Risk, *Econometrica*, 47, 277.

Kahneman, D., B. L. Fredrickson, C. A. Schreiber, and D. A. Redelmeier (1993). "When More Pain Is Preferred to Less: Adding a Better End," *Psychological Science*, 4, 401–405.

Lunenburg, F. C. (2010). "Escalation of Commitment: Patterns of Retrospective Rationality," *International Journal of Management, Business, and Administration*, vol. 13 (1) 2010.

Maslow, A. H. (1943). "A Theory of Human Motivation," *Psychological Review*, 50, 370–396.

Maslow, A. H. (1954). "Motivation and Personality."

Poundstone, W.. (2010). "Priceless: The Myth of Fair Value (and How to Take Advantage of It)."

Shafir, E., I. Simonson, and A. Tversky (1993). "Reason-Based Choice," *Cognition* 49, 11–36.

Slovic, P. and S. Lichtenstein (1968). "Relative Importance of Probabilities and Payoffs in Risk Taking," *Journal of Experimental Psychology*, vol. 78 (3, pt.2), Nov. 1968, 1–18.

Stevens, S. S. (1975). "Psychophysics: Introduction to Its Perceptual, Neural, and Social Prospects."

Thaler, R. H. (1985). "Mental Accounting and Consumer Choice." *Marketing Science* 4, 199–214, 209.

Tversky, A., E. Shafir (1992). "Choice under Conflict: The Dynamics of Deferred Decision," *Psychological Science*, 3, 358–361.

wgbh educational foundation (undated). "Before You Buy An Suv ... ," retrieved at http://www.pbs.org/wgbh/pages/frontline/shows/rollover/etc/before.html on Dec. 15, 2012.

Ziegenhagen, M. (2011). "Software Pricing," Speech at Haas Business School, University of California at Berkeley, Mar. 2, 2011.

Chapter: Attraction

Ariely, D. (2008). "Predictably Irrational: The Hidden Forces That Shape Our Decisions."

Ariely, D. (2010). "The Upside of Irrationality: The Unexpected Benefits of Defying Logic at Work and at Home."

Ariely, D. and G. Loewenstein (2006). "The Heat of the Moment: The Effect of Sexual Arousal on Sexual Decision Making," *Journal of Behavioral Decision Making*, vol. 19, 87–98.

Asch, S. E. (1951). "Effects of Group Pressure on the Modification and Distortion of Judgements," in: H. Guetzkow (Ed.), "Groups, leadership and men", 177–190.

Bateson, M., D. Nettle, and G. Roberts (2006). "Cues of Being Watched Enhance Cooperation in a Real-World Setting," *Biology Letters*, 2 (3), Sept. 2006, 412–414.

Beckwith, H. (2011). "Unthinking – the Surprising Forces behind What We Buy."

Berneman, C., and R. Reeler (1986). "Shoppers' Mood and Purchases," Paper presented at ASAC Conference, June 2–5, Vancouver, BC, Canada (quoted from: Hill, R. P., and M. P. Gardner (1987): The Buying Process: Effects of and on Consumer Mood States, *Advances in Consumer Research*, vol. 14, 1987, 408–410.)

Bertrand, M., D. Karlan, S. Mullainathan, E. Shafir, and J. Zinman (2010). "What Is Advertising Content Worth? Evidence from a Consumer Credit Marketing Field Experiment*," *Quarterly Journal of Economics*, 125 (1), 2010, 263–305.

Choi, C. Q. (2005). "About Face," *Scientific American*, Aug. 2005, 16.

Cole, S. (2009). "Less Product, Same Price," *Marketplace*, Jan. 8, 2009, retrieved at http://www.marketplace.org/topics/life/less-product-same-price?refid=0 on Feb. 29, 2012.

Cunningham, K. (2012). "Do Chick-Magnets Really Work? Corvettes, Testosterone & Peahens," *Beyond the Purchase Blog*, retrieved at http://www.beyondthepurchase.org/blog/08/do-chick-magnets-really-work-corvettes-testosterone-peahens/ on Dec. 16, 2012.

Cunningham, K. (2012). "Men Are from Mercedes. Women Are from Versace," *Beyond the Purchase Blog*, retrieved at http://www.beyondthepurchase.org/blog/09/men-are-from-mercedes-women-are-from-versace/ on Dec. 16, 2012.

Cunningham, K. (2012). "She's Not Looking at You: What Really Inspires a Woman to Go Shopping," *Beyond the Purchase Blog*, retrieved at http://www.beyondthepurchase.org/blog/09/shes-not-looking-at-you-what-really-inspires-a-woman-to-go-shopping/ on Dec. 16, 2012.

DePaulo, P. J. (1985). "The 'Addictive' Potential of Non-Drug Products," Working Paper (quoted from Hill, R.P., and M. P. Gardner (1987)).

DePaulo, P. J. (1986). "The Opposite of Satiation: Motivational Priming as an Aftereffect of a Pleasurable Consumption Experience," *Advances in Consumer Research*, vol. XIII, 192–197.

Dominy, N. J. and P. W. Lucas (2001). "Ecological Importance of Trichromatic Vision to Primates," *Nature* 410, 363–66.

Ferriss, T. (2007). "The 4-Hour Workweek: Escape 9-5, Live Anywhere, and Join the New Rich."

Gorzelany, J. (2012). "Cars With the Most Brand-Loyal Buyers," *Forbes* Oct. 10, 2012, retrieved at http://www.forbes.com/sites/jimgorzelany/2012/10 /10/cars-delivering-the-most-brand-loyal-buyers/print/ on Jan. 18, 2013.

Gossen, H. H. (1854). "Entwickelung der Gesetze des menschlichen Verkehrs und der daraus fließenden Regeln für menschliches Handeln."

Haag, M. (2009). "The Templars: The History and the Myth: From Solomon's Temple to the Freemasons."

Harrison, P. (2007). "In Oxytocin We Trust," Aug. 31, 2007, retrieved at http://tribalinsight.wordpress.com/2007/08/31/in-oxytocin-we-trust/ on Feb. 26, 2012.

Harrison, P. (2008). "The Science of Supermarket Psychology," retrieved at http://tribalinsight.wordpress.com/2008/08/19/supe rmarket-psychology/ on Mar. 28, 2013.

Hill, G. (2012). "The Experience of Awe: Purchasing Experiences Can Produce Emotional Benefits," Oct. 5, 2012, retrieved at http://www.prweb.com/releases/happy_to_be/awe/ prweb9972935.htm on Dec. 12, 2012.

Hofman, D., and S. Aronow (2012): The Gartner Supply Chain Top 25 for 2012, G00234062, May 21, 2012.

Huebner, G. (2012). "Danone" Speech at Campus for Sales at WHU Otto Beisheim School of Management by Sales Director Germany, Danone GmbH, Feb. 10, 2012.

Isbell, L. A. (2006). "Snakes as Agents of Evolutionary Change in Primate Brains," *Journal of Human Evolution*, 51, 1–35.

Jameson, K. A., S. M. Highnote, and Linda M. Wasserman (2001). "Richer Color Experience in Observers with Multiple Photopigment Opsin Genes," *Psychonomic Bulletin and Review*, 8 (2), 244–61.

Kahneman, D. (2012). "Thinking Fast and Slow."

Kaku, M. (2011). "Physics of the Future."

Keller, A. (2007). "The Art of the Aisle," Florida Trend, Oct. 1, 2007.

Keltner, D. (2009). "Born to Be Good: The Science of a Meaningful Life."

Lehrer, J. (2011). "Ads Implant False Memories." *Wired*, May 2011

Li, Y. J., D. T. Kenrick, V. Griskevicius, and S. L. Neuberg (2011). "Economic Biases in Evolutionary Perspective: How Mating and Self-Protection Motives Alter Loss Aversion," *Journal of Personality and Social Psychology*, vol. 102 (3), Mar. 2012, 550–561.

Loftus, E. F. (1997). Creating False Memories, *Scientific American*, Sept. 1997, 70-75.

Lossau, N. (2012). "Neuer Ton beim TV," *Die Welt*, June 2, 2012, 24.

Luntz, F. I. (2009). "What Americans Really Want ... Really: The Truth about Our Hopes, Dreams, and Fears."

Mandel, N., and E. J. Johnson (2002). When Web Pages Influence Choice: Effects of Visual Primes on Experts and Novices (Sept. 2002), *Journal of Consumer Research*, vol. 29 (2), 2002.

Müller, M. U. (2012). "Der Weg ist das Ziel," *Der Spiegel*, Jan. 9, 2012, 72–74.

Müller, W. (2011). "Die richtige Vorsorge für Ihren Typ," in: Focus Money 14/2011, 5.

Nader, K. and E. Ö. Einarsson (2010). Memory Reconsolidation: An Update, *Annals of the New York Academy of Sciences*, 1191:27–41.

Pariser, E. (2011). The Filter Bubble.

Pease, A., and B. Pease (2006). "The Definitive Book of Body Language."

Poundstone, W. (2010). "Priceless: The Myth of Fair Value (and How to Take Advantage of It)."

Rajagopal, P. and N. Votolato Montgomery (2011). "I Imagine, I Experience, I Like: The False Experience Effect," *Journal of Consumer Research* vol. 38 (3), Oct. 2011.

Reißmann, O.(2010). "Psychoprofile alarmieren Verbraucherschützer," *Der Spiegel*, Nov. 4, 2010.

Schuman, E. (2006). "Self-Checkout Killing Impulse Items," *eWeek*, July 25, 2006.

Schwertfeger, B. (2012). "Die großen Business Schools sind lebendige Leichen," *SpiegelOnline*, Sept. 2, 2012, retrieved at http://www.spiegel.de/karriere/berufsleben/0,1518,8 13654,00.html on Sept. 14, 2012.

Sethi, R. (2009). "I Will Teach You to Be Rich."

Slovic, P. (1975). Choice between Equally Valued Alternatives, *Journal of Experimental Psychology: Human Perception and Performance*, I, 280–287.

Tanz, J. (2012). "The Curse of Cow Clicker," *Wired* magazine, Jan. 2012.

University College London (2006). Irrational Decisions Driven by Emotions, *ScienceDaily*, Aug. 3, 2006, retrieved at http://www.sciencedaily.com/releases/2006/08/0608 03171138.htm on Apr. 6, 2013.

Unknown (2012). "10 Best Super Bowl 2012 Commercials," retrieved on http://www.superbowl-commercials.org/14261.html as of June 7, 2012.

Unknown (2009). "Swedish Jeans 'Made in North Korea' Go on Sale," *the Independent*, Dec. 21, 2009.

Welch, J. (2005). "Winning."

Chapter: Pricing Rationales

Andersen, S., S. Ertaç, U. Gneezy, M. Hoffman, and J. A. List (2011). "Stakes Matter in Ultimatum Games," *American Economic Review*, 101 (7): 3427–39.

Ariely, D. (2008). "Predictably Irrational: The Hidden Forces That Shape Our Decisions."

Bazerman, M. H., S. B. White, and G. F. Loewenstein (1995). "Perceptions of Fairness in Interpersonal and Individual Choice Situations," *Current Directions in Psychological Science*, 4, 39–43.

Carter, Z., J. Cherkis, and R. Grim (2012). Mitt Romney Haunted by Missing Tax Returns as Campaign Draws to Close, Nov. 6, 2012, retrieved at http://www.huffingtonpost.com/2012/11/05/mitt-romney-missing-tax-returns_n_2079903.html on Mar. 1, 2013.

Dolan, R. J. (2003). "Pricing: A Value-Based Approach," *Harvard Business School*, 9-500-071, Nov. 3, 2003.

Hinterhuber, A., and S. Liozu (Eds.) (2012). "Innovation in Pricing: Contemporary Theories and Best Practices."

Hoffman, E., K. A. McCabe, K. Shachat, and V. L. Smith (1994). "Preferences, Property Rights, and Anonymity in Bargaining Games," *Games and Economic Behavior* 7, 346–380.

Hoffman, E., K. A. McCabe, and V. L. Smith (1996). "On Expectations and the Monetary Stakes in Ultimatum Games," *International Journal of Game Theory*, 25, 289–301.

Kahnemann, D., and A. Tversky (1979). "Prospect Theory: An Analysis of Decision under Risk," *Econometrica*, 47, 263–292.

Kahneman, D., J. Knetsch, and R. Thaler (1986). Fairness and the Assumption of Economics, *Journal of Business*, vol 59 (4, pt. 2), *The Behavioral Foundation of Economics*, S285–S300.

Mlodinow, L. (2009). "The Drunkard's Walk: How Randomness Rules Our Lives."

Niederlich, R. (2008). "Kraftstoff-Test Shell V-Power 95," *AutoBild*, Nov. 10, 2008, retrieved http://www.autobild.de/artikel/kraftstoff-test-shell-v-power-95-804732.html on Mar, 28, 2013.

Poundstone, W. (2010). "Priceless: The Myth of Fair Value (and How to Take Advantage of It)."

Ritov, I. (1996). Anchoring in a Simulated Competitive Market Negotiation, *Organizational Behavior and Human Decision Processes*, 67, 16–25.

Sam (2008). "The True Price of SMS Messages," retrieved at http://gthing.net/the-true-price-of-sms-messages on Apr. 7, 2012.

Simon, H. (2008). "The Impact of Academic Research on Business Practice: Experiences from Marketing," *Journal of Business Market Management*, 2, 203–18, 214.

Sundem, G. (2012). "A Fun DIY Science Goodie: The Behavioral Economics of Agreement (and Why Negotiations Fail)," *Scientific American*, Apr. 5, 2012, retrieved at http://blogs.scientificamerican.com/guest-blog/2012/04/05/a-fun-diy-science-goodie-the-behavioral-economics-of-agreement-and-why-negotiations-fail/ on April 7, 2012.

Chapter: Relativity and Fix Points

Ariely, D. (2008). "Predictably Irrational: The Hidden Forces That Shape Our Decisions."

Ariely, D., G. Loewenstein, and D. Prelec (2003). "Coherent Arbitrariness: Stable Demand Curves without Stable Preferences," *The Quarterly Journal of Economics*, 118, 73–105.

Arndt, R. Z. (2011). "Gilded Grub/ Burger Shoppe's $175 Burger," *Fast Company*, July 1, 2011.

Binkley, C. (2007). "The Psychology of the $14,000 Handbag," *Wall Street Journal*, Aug 9, 2007.

Chapman, G. B., and B. H. Bornstein (1996). "The More You Ask for, the More You Get: Anchoring in Personal Injury Verdicts," *Applied Cognitive Psychology*, 10, 519–40.

Ciotti, G. (2012). "Using Behavioral Economics, Psychology, and Neuroeconomics to Maximize Sales," retrieved at http://www.shopify.com/blog/6563013-using-behavioral-economics-psychology-and-neuroeconomics-to-maximize-sales on Sept. 21, 2012.

Della Bitta, A. J. and K. B. Monroe (1974). "The Influence of Adaptation Levels on Subjective Price Perceptions," *Advances in Consumer Research*, vol. 1, 359–369.

Fickenscher, L. (2011). "Bankruptcy for NYC Eatery Selling $175 Burgers," *Crain's New York Business*, July 6, 2011.

Guthrie, C., and D. Orr (2006). "Anchoring, Information, Expertise, and Negotiation: New Insights from Meta-Analysis," *Ohio State Journal on Dispute Resolution*; Vanderbilt Law and Economics Research Paper No. 06-12.

Hublot (2012). "BaselWorld 2012," Press Release.

Huber, J., and C. Puto (1983). "Market Boundaries and Product Choice: Illustrating Attraction and Substitution Effects," *Journal of Consumer Research*, 10, 31–44.

Malouff, J., and N. S. Schutte (1989). "Shaping Juror Attitutes: Effects of Requesting Different Damage Amounts in Personal Injury Trials," *The Journal of Social Psychology*, 129, 491–495.

Mussweiler, T. (2001). "The Durability of Anchoring Effects," *European Journal of Social Psychology*, 31: 431–442.

Mussweiler, T., F. Strack, and T. Pfeiffer (2000). "Overcoming the Inevitable Anchoring Effect: Considering the Opposite Compensates for Selective Accessibility," *Personality and Social Psychology Bulletin* 26, Nov. 2000. 1142–1150.

Norcraft, G. B., and M. A. Neale (1987). "Experts, Amateurs, and Real Estate — an Anchoring-and-Adjustment Perspective on Property Pricing Decisions," *Organizational Behavior and Human Decision Processes*, 39, 84–97.

Plous, Sc. (1993). "The Psychology of Judgment and Decision Making."

Poundstone, W. (2010). "Priceless: The Myth of Fair Value (and How to Take Advantage of It)."

Simonson, I., and A.Tversky (1992). "Choice in Context: Tradeoff Contrast and Extremeness Aversion," *Journal of Marketing Research*, 29, 281–95.

Shafir, E., I. Simonson, and A. Tversky (1993). "Reason-Based Choice," *Cognition*, 49, 11–36.

Tversky, A., and D. Kahnemann (1974). "Judgement under Uncertainty: Heuristics and Biases," *Science*, 185, 453–58.

Simonsohn, U., and G. F. Loewenstein (2006). "Mistake #37: The Effect of Previously Encountered Prices on Current Housing Demand," *Economic Journal*, vol. 116 (508), Jan. 2006, 175–199.

Timothy D. W., C. Houston, K. Etling, and N. Brekke (1996). "A New Look at Anchoring Effects:

Basic Anchoring and Its Antecedents," *Journal of Experimental Psychology: General*, 4, 387–402.

Chapter: Differentiation

Amster-Burton, M. (2010). "Hungry Monkey: A Food-Loving Father's Quest to Raise an Adventurous Eater."

Amster-Burton, M. (2012). "Would You Like That Meal Bundled, or Unbundled," *mintlife blog*, retrieved at http://www.mint.com/blog/consumer-iq/would-you-like-that-meal-bundled-or-unbundled-012012/ on Mar. 23, 2012.

Ariely, D. (2008). "Predictably Irrational: The Hidden Forces That Shape Our Decisions."

Chamberlin, E. (1933). "The Theory of Monopolistic Competition: A Re-Orientation of the Theory of Value."

Channel 9 ABC (2012). "Consumer Reports: Using too much detergent?" retrieved at http://www.9wsyr.com/content/consumers/story/Consumer-Reports-Using-too-much-detergent/BelJi8vP-ku_hmck0AgFAQ.cspx, on Feb. 13, 2012.

Cole, S. (2009). "Less Product, Same Price," in Marketplace.

Consumer Reports, Jan. 2009, 63, retrieved at http://www.consumerreports.org/cro/selling/selling-it/selling-it-ov.htm on Mar. 31, 2013.

Courty, P., and M. Pagliero (2009). "The Impact of Price Differentiation on Revenue. Evidence from the Concert Industry," Working Paper No. 105.

Gossen, H. H. (1854). "Entwickelung der Gesetze des menschlichen Verkehrs und der daraus fließenden Regeln für menschliches Handeln."

Guenther, H. G. (2003). "Clever Möbel kaufen."

Iyer, G. (2011). "Product Line Pricing and Bundling," Speech at Haas Business School University of California at Berkeley, Mar. 2, 2011.

Kahneman, D., J. Knetsch, and R. Thaler. (1986). "Fairness and the Assumption of Economics," *The Journal of Business*, vol. 59 (4, pt. 2): *The Behavioral Foundation of Economics*, S285–S300.

Kalwani, M. U., C. K. Yim, H. J. Rinne, and Y. Sugita (1990). "A Price Expectations Model of customer Brand Choice," *Journal of Marketing Research*.

Kelso, A. (Ed) (2005). "Engineering a Better Menu," retrieved at http://www.pizzamarketplace.com/article/109167/Engineering-a-better-menu on Mar. 20, 2012.

Png, I. P. L., and H. Wang (2008). "Buyer Uncertainty and Two-Part Pricing: Theory with Evidence from Outsourcing and New York Restaurants," Working Paper, Mar. 2008.

Porter, E. (2011). "The Price of Everything."

Sharpe, K. M., and R. Staelin (2010). "Consumption Effects of Bundling: Consumer Perceptions, Firm Actions, and Public Policy Implications," *Journal of Public Policy and Marketing*, vol. 29 (2), Fall 2010.

Thaler, R. H. (1985). "Mental Accounting and Consumer Choice," *Marketing Science*, 4, 199–214.

Walls, C. (2009). "How to Sell More Toothpaste."

Ziegenhagen, M. (2011). "Software Pricing," Speech at Haas Business School University of California at Berkeley, Mar. 2, 2011.

Chapter: Trojan Free

Ariely, D. (2008). "Predictably Irrational: The Hidden Forces That Shape Our Decisions."

CASPIAN (2001). "CASPIAN Shoppers Discuss Kroger 'Card Savings,'" retrieved at http://www.nocards.org/savings/savingsletterskroger.shtml on Sept. 16, 2012.

Kahnemann, D. and A. Tversky (1979). "Prospect Theory: An Analysis of Decision Under Risk," *Econometrica*, 47, 263–292.

Kwok, J. (2011). "Girl in Translation."

Mauss, M.(1954). "The Gift: Forms and Functions of Exchange in Archaic Societies."

Norton, M. I., Daniel Mochon, and Dan Ariely (2011). "The 'IKEA Effect': When Labor Leads to Love," *Harvard Business School*, Working Paper 11-091.

Porter, E. (2011). "The Price of Everything."

Unknown (2011). "McDonald's Credit Card Payments," Mar. 30, 2011, retrieved at http://www.consumer.org.nz/news/view/mcdonalds-credit-card-payments on Sept. 16, 2012.

Veen, G. (2005). "Fat Free Water," retrieved at http://www.veen.com/greg/archives/000801.html on Aug. 31, 2012.

Wikipedia (2012). "The Big Texan Steak Ranch," retrieved at http://en.wikipedia.org/wiki/The_Big_Texan_Steak_Ranch on Mar. 10, 2012.

Chapter: Discounts

Beks (2011). "Do You Groupon?" retrieved at http://www.bloggingawaydebt.com/2011/07/do-you-groupon/ on July 25, 2011.

Conner, P. (2012). "Behavioral Economics: What It Is and Three Ways Marketers Can Use It," *Quirk's Marketing Research Review*, Mar. 2012, retrieved at http://www.quirks.com/articles/2012/20120326-1.aspx on Apr. 8, 2012.

Parks Associates (2012). "Bargain Hunters," *Inc.*, Apr. 2012, 30.

Nielsen (2012). "Holiday Shopping," *Inc.*, Dec. 2011/Jan. 2012, 32.

US Census Bureau (2006). "Personal income for all sexes, races in 2005," retrieved at http://en.wikipedia.org/wiki/Personal_income_in_th e_United_States on Nov. 19, 2006.

Grow, B. (2005). "The Great Rebate Runaround," *BusinessWeek*, Nov. 23, 2005.

Sethi, R. (2009). "I Will Teach You to Be Rich."

Thaler, R. H. (1985). "Mental Accounting and Consumer Choice," Marketing Science 4, 199–214.

Granger, D. (2011). "Paying Retail," *Esquire*, Dec. 2011.

Porter, E. (2011). "The Price of Everything."

Liang, J., and V. Kanetkar (2006). "Price Endings: Magic and Math," *Journal of Product and Brand Management*, vol. 15 (6), 377–385.

Anderson, E. T. and D. Simester (2003). "Effects of $9 Price Endings on Retail Sales: Evidence from Field Experiments," *Quantitative Marketing and Economics*, 1(1): 93–110.

Tversky, A., and D. Kahneman (1981). "The Framing of Decisions and the Psychology of Choice," *Science 211*, 453–58, 459.

Chapter: Fooling Around

Anderson, C. K., and X. Xie (2010). "Pricing and Market Segmentation Using Opaque Selling Mechanisms," submission for the Airline Group of the International Federation of Operational Research Societies annual award

Courty, P., and W. Liu (2013). "Opaque Selling: Static or Inter-Temporal Price Discrimination," March. 2013, retrieved at http://web.uvic.ca/~pcourty/OpaquePricing.pdf on June 23, 2013.

Langer, E., A. Blank, and B. Chanowitz (1978). "The Mindlessness of Ostensibly Thoughtful Action: The Role of "Placebic" Information in Interpersonal Interaction," *Journal of Personality and Social Psychology*, 36 (6), 635–642.

Chapter: Making It Happen
Ariely, D., and K. Wertenbroch (2002). "Procrastination, Deadlines, and Performance: Self-Control by Precommitment," *Psychological Science*, 2002.

Baumeister, R. (2012). "Willpower: Rediscovering the Greatest Human Strength."

Baumeister, R., et al. (1998). "Ego Depletion: Is the Active Self a Limited Resource?" *Journal of Personality and Social Psychology*, vol. 74 (5), 1998, 1252–1265.

Carey, B. (2007). "Who's Minding the Mind?" in: *New York Times*, July 31, 2007, retrieved at http://www.nytimes.com/2007/07/31/health/psychology/31subl.html?_r=1 on Mar. 4, 2012.

Ferriss, T. (2010). "The 4-Hour Body: An Uncommon Guide to Rapid Fat-Loss, Incredible Sex, and Becoming Superhuman."

Rogov, K. and C. M. Reinhart (2011). "This Time Is Different: Eight Centuries of Financial Folly."